Ulrike Müller

The New Cat Handbook

Care, Nutrition, Diseases, and Breeding of Cats

With a Special Chapter on Cat Language by Paul Leyhausen

Color Photographs by Outstanding Animal Photographers and Drawings by Fritz W. Köhler

Translated from the German by Rita and Robert Kimber

American Advisory Editor Matthew M. Vriends, Ph.D.

CHILDRENS PRESS CHOICE
A Barron's title selected for educational distribution
ISBN 0-516-08683-9

Cover pictures
Front cover. Long-haired house cat.
Back cover. Above: Young ocelot; black and white
Persian; house cat carrying her kitten.
Middle: House cat kittens; house cat with tiger
markings.
Below: Brown tabby Persian; house cat kittens.
Inside front cover. House cat kittens, one black and
white, one with tiger markings.
Inside back cover. Norwegian Forest Cat, tabby
with white.

First English language edition published in 1984 by
Barron's Educational Series, Inc.

Originally published in German under the title *Das
Neue Katzenbuch*
© 1984 by Gräfe und Unzer GmbH, Munchen,
West Germany

All inquiries should be addressed to: Barron's
Educational Series, Inc., 113 Crossways Park
Drive, Woodbury, New York 11797

International Standard Book No. 0-8120-2922-4

PRINTED IN HONG KONG

6   490   9 8 7 6

Book Credits
Hans Scherz, series editor
Doris Schimmelpfennig-Funke, volume editor
Heinz Kraxenberger, cover designer

Photo Credits
Angermeyer/Tierpark Hellabrunn: page 56 (below
right); Animal/Thompson: pages 73 (below left) and
110 (middle left); Adriaanse: pages 37 (below right),
38 (above left, above right, below), 92, 127 (below
left); Bruin: pages 10 (above left), 91 (above and
below); Gautschi: page 128 (above); Hinz: pages 109,
110 (below left and right), inside back cover; Dr.
Jesse: back cover (above left); Layer: page 20 (middle
right); Meyers: page 56 (middle left); Reinhard: inside
front cover, pages 10 (below left and right), 20 (above
left and right, middle left, below left and right), 56
(above left, below left), 74, 110 (above left, middle
right), 127 (above left and right, middle left and right,
below right), 128 (below), back cover (above right,
middle right); Röhl-Herrlich: page 19; Scherz: page 73
(above); Schmidecker: page 56 (above right);
Skogstad: front cover, pages 37 (above left and right,
middle left and right, below left), 73 (below right), 110
(above right), back cover (middle, below left);
Ullmann: back cover (below right); Wegler: pages 9,
10 (above right); Wothe: pages 55 (above, below), 56
(middle right).

The drawings accompanying the special chapter
"Cat Language" are based on photographs and
drawings in Professor Leyhausen's book *Cat
Behavior (Katzen — eine Verhaltenskunde)*,
published by Garland STPM Press, New York,
1979.

Ulrike Müller
The author lives with her husband, a
veterinarian, on Lahn Valley Farm near the
university town of Marburg in Hessen, West
Germany. Ms. Müller has been breeding purebred
cats for many years, and cats she has bred and
raised number among the top animals shown at
international competitions. Ms. Müller frequently
travels to competitions in other countries to serve as
a judge.

Contents

Contents

Contents

Preface

There is no shortage of information and well-intentioned advice on how to keep cats. Nonetheless, anyone trying to find clear answers will have a hard time because very often different sources contradict each other—even in questions that have been definitively answered by the sciences of ethology, animal nutrition, and veterinary medicine. Some of the things anyone who has cats would like to know are: Does a tomcat absolutely have to be neutered? Is it better to give a cat commercial food or other food, or should I alternate between the two? What can I do if my cat keeps having diarrhea? Are there diseases that can be communicated from cats to humans? Are cats loners, as people often say, or are they happier if they have company of their own kind?

The New Cat Handbook will give you the right answers. Three experts — each competent in his or her field — explain everything a cat owner may want to know about keeping cats, cat diseases, behavior, and the breeding of cats. Ulrike Müller has had cats since childhood; she keeps ordinary house cats as well as pedigreed cats, has been breeding Siamese and Birman cats for years, and travels all over the world to judge cats at exhibitions. She draws on her long practical experience with cats in giving advice on keeping and caring for cats, in explaining the basic facts of genetics in layperson's terms, in discussing the topic of "Breeding Cats," and in introducing many breeds of pedigreed cats.

With her husband, who is a veterinarian, she has written the chapter dealing with cat diseases and preventive health care. The information and advice in these sections is probably as comprehensive and complete as that offered by any other books on cats, if not more so.

The many varied elements of expression that make up "Cat Language" are discussed by Professor Paul Leyhausen who has been observing the behavior of different kinds of cats in the context of scientific studies. He shows how cats, with their great expressive range, communicate not only with each other and with members of other species but also with humans. Anyone who reads carefully the chapter Professor Leyhausen has written will gain new insights and a better understanding of cats.

The illustrations are factual and informative, but they capture at the same time all the beauty and fascination our house cats and pedigreed cats emanate. Sixty color photographs depict the most common types of house cats, the colorations most often seen in purebred cats, and some large and small members of the cat family that live in the wild. The drawings illustrate some common behavior patterns of cats, often showing them in successive frames that bring out details otherwise hidden from the human eye.

The history of this book's origin is just as unusual as much that it contains. The publishers asked cat owners in a questionnaire what aspects of keeping cats they were most interested in, and the book grew out of their responses. What resulted is an attractive, practical book, a resource that contains all the information cat lovers really need.

The author and the publishers would like to thank everyone who has had a share in the making of this book: the cat owners who filled out and returned the questionnaires, the animal photographers who let us use their best pictures, and the artist Fritz W. Köhler, who provided such expressive drawings. We also thank H. Alfred Müller, D.V.M., for his advice on the chapter about health care and the diseases of cats and Professor Paul Leyhausen for his contribution on "Cat Language" and for checking the entire manuscript.

Considerations Before You Get a Cat

Before you set out to get a cat, you should be fully aware that you are about to take on responsibility for another creature, that you will have to spend time with the cat, and that its upkeep costs money. This is true whether the animal in question is a relatively independent house cat or a pedigreed cat whose care will be more time-consuming. To have a relationship that is mutually satisfying, you have to do more than just fill the cat's dish, pet the cat briefly, clean out the litter box, and disappear. To be happy, a cat needs your affection, especially if it is kept exclusively indoors. An apartment cat is bound to feel lonely if you live alone, have a job, and perhaps spend many evening and weekend hours away from home. Every cat depends not only on daily feeding but also on a daily chat or play session.

If you are not prepared to spend much time on a cat, I advise you urgently not to get *one* cat. But this does not mean that you have to do without feline company. On the contrary, you should get *two* kittens, preferably litter mates that are already used to playing together.

We call it "rubbing up" when a cat rubs its cheek or neck against any accessible part of its human friend.

Are you a relaxed, patient person, or will you become frantic if your kitten decides to do acrobatics on your curtains, dig in the flower pots, nibble on house plants, or knock over and smash a valuable vase? Will it bother you if upholstered furniture and wallpaper show the wear and tear of cats or if you find cat hair on carpets, tables, clothes, and perhaps in your soup? If you think you can put up with all these minor annoyances calmly, then a cat will be happy in your home.

Ordinary House Cat or Pedigreed Cat?

As much as cats of different breeds vary in shape and color, there are very few character traits that can be linked to breed. Individuals of a certain breed often exhibit common qualities of spirit and temperament, but animals of different breeds can resemble each other in these respects just as much.

Most cat lovers respond to cats regardless of differences in breed and color, although they may have personal preferences. Each person should choose the cat that best meets his or her fancy. It happens very frequently that cat lovers acquire their pets quite by accident, often by coming across a stray. Most of them soon consider their particular cat unique and would not dream of giving it up, though they might have described it as ugly before.

As a general rule one can say that sedate Persians put up better with being left alone part of the time in a small apartment than the generally more temperamental and enterprising Siamese and Orientals. However, long-haired cats require more time for grooming than others.

The best choice, if you live in a city apartment without access to the outdoors, is a quiet long-haired cat. If you have a house with a garden, a lively Siamese will be happy there, whereas a tough, ordinary house cat is best suited for chasing mice on a farm.

Considerations Before You Get a Cat

Of course, there are no hard and fast rules about which type of cat has to be kept in an apartment, which in a house in the suburbs, and which on a farm in the countryside except for the common-sense one that a long-haired cat should not be expected to fend for itself in the country like a barn cat without care and grooming.

The Cost of Purchase and Care

There are plenty of opportunities to acquire kittens at no cost. Cat owners are often only too happy to find good homes for their kittens.

If you decide to get a cat from an animal shelter, you usually have to pay for vaccinations and for neutering the cat. Young pedigreed cats, on the other hand, can cost several hundred dollars.

The price of pedigreed cats depends not only on the breed — different breeds vary considerably in cost — but also on whether the cat is of show caliber. It would be a simple matter if a high price or renowned ancestry guaranteed show quality. But this is not the case, and it is extremely hard to tell whether a twelve-week-old kitten is going to turn into a champion or whether it will never be more than a nice pet. There are pedigreed kittens that look very promising but never develop their apparent potential, and there are ugly ducklings among kittens that grow into stunning swans.

The purchase price is not the only money you will have to spend on your kitten. You will also need to buy initial equipment, for which you can pay anywhere from a few to over a hundred dollars. The cost of food will range somewhere between $15 and $30 a month, and there will be a veterinarian's bill for the necessary vaccinations. If the cat gets sick, there will be further bills for treatment

and medications. The following figures are estimates, but will give you an idea of the annual cost of a cat: Food and accessories, $130; veterinary care, $100 to $250; boarding, $5 to $10 per day; kitty litter, $80.

Keeping a Cat in a Rented Apartment

Before you decide to get a cat, you should read over your lease. If there is any doubt whether pets are allowed in your building, I would urge you to get written permission from your landlord. If sound travels easily in the building, you should keep in mind that the loud meowing of a cat in heat can be a considerable nuisance for your neighbors.

Insuring Your Cat

If you are buying a particularly valuable cat, you may want to get an insurance policy that covers veterinary treatment in case of illness and/or reimburses you for the value of the animal in case of loss. Your normal liability policy protects you against any damage caused by your cat to persons and property: biting, tearing clothes, injuring or killing other animals like chickens, dogs, or pigeons, etc.

Havanna Brown cat with tiger-striped kitten. ▷
The Havanna Brown is an Oriental Shorthair that is sometimes described as a "Siamese in unicolored dress."

Considerations Before You Get a Cat

Female or Male?

I have never observed any sex-linked character differences in my cats. I have raised both males and females that were exceptionally loving and cuddly. Other kittens of both sexes developed into little "wildcats." Even later, when you consider having your cat neutered, sex plays no major role (page 83). Older cats and neutered cats of both sexes are often especially affectionate.

A Cat for Your Child?

Cats are by nature very sensitive and often have marked personalities. They hate coercion, rough handling, hasty movements, and above all loud noises and banging. Most cats like to spend much of their time — about two thirds of the day — resting quietly and peacefully. For these reasons it is not a good idea to get a cat for a small child. A pet with more modest demands and a less complex psyche (a guinea pig, for example) is a better choice under these conditions. Still, cats and children, even young ones, can coexist happily and enjoy each other if the parents teach the children how to treat their pet and if they make sure the cat's needs are not violated. Older children can gradually take over the

◁ Oriental Shorthairs and Siamese.
Above left: Oriental Shorthair, black and silver spotted.
Above right: Siamese Tabby-point with kitten.
Below left: Oriental Shorthair Blue, kittens black and blue.
Below right: Siamese Foreign White and Siamese Seal-point.

responsibilities of looking after the cat if it gives them pleasure and if they express a desire to do so. For most children, being around a cat is a particularly good way to learn to respect animals and their personalities.

Vacation Care

Plan ahead who will look after your cat when you want to go away on vacation. In some cities there are cat sitters' clubs where you can find someone willing to tend your cat, even in your own apartment if you wish. Cats suffer if they are taken out of their familiar surroundings and separated from "their" people, and they are more likely to get sick at these times. If you do have to take your cat to a boarding shelter, make sure the animal's vaccination record is up to date. Also, look the shelter over beforehand and discuss the needs of your animal with the owners. Some shelters do not accept unneutered male cats.

How and Where to Find a Cat

Choosing a House Cat
Ordinarily, you do not have to look long to find a house cat. In the countryside particularly, there are almost always unwanted kittens and people eager to find homes for them. In the city you can go to one of the many animal shelters where there are plenty of cats eagerly awaiting release from their miserable situation.

Wherever you acquire your cat, be it from a farm, from friends, or from a shelter, have your veterinarian look it over.

Considerations Before You Get a Cat

Stray Cats

You may run across an apparently homeless cat on a walk or excursion in the countryside. Some of these animals are rather shy and reserved; others are very friendly. It may happen that a cat will adopt you and keep following you. If it is a tame, well-fed kitten, chances are that it has a home nearby and is only temporarily out on its own. You should never take such an animal along without having made thorough inquiries about where it might belong.

If a cat looks thin and ragged, it is more likely to be a real stray.

If you take your cat in your lap, it will start "kneading." This behavior goes back to the days of kittenhood, when these paw movements stimulated the flow of mother's milk.

If a cat hangs around your house obviously on the lookout for a new source of food, you are probably correct in assuming that it either was abandoned or escaped on a trip in unfamiliar surroundings.

There is generally no reason not to adopt such a creature. If it is fully grown, tame, and well cared for, you may try to find its owner by placing an ad in your local newspaper.

Once you have decided to keep the stray, you should take it to a veterinarian for vaccinations and a health check.

Buying a Pedigreed Cat

These days it is possible to get pedigreed cats through the mail, but you should never buy a cat that way. Cat clubs and societies will be happy to give you addresses of breeders or arrange a purchase for you. For only a small fee, the Cat Fanciers' Association (CFA) will send you a directory of the more than 3,000 cat breeders throughout the United States. Pet sections of department stores also offer pedigreed cats for sale. If you are interested in buying a cat of a certain breed or a show animal, you had best get in touch with a cat association (addresses, page 141) which will assist you not only with the purchase but also with any problems or questions you may have later.

There are a few breeders who belong to a recognized association but still pursue their business primarily for pecuniary motives. That is why it is best if you can have a look yourself to see if the animals are kept properly and raised with love and affection. Cats should have plenty of light, air, and space, as well as opportunities for playing and climbing and contact with people and other cats.

Sometimes a breeder may not have a cat of the desired breed. In the case of some unusual varieties, there may be a waiting period of two or more years for obtaining a kitten.

Another source of a pedigreed cat of your choice is cat shows.

If your kitten is imported from another country, the seller is obliged to furnish you with the following papers:

Considerations Before You Get a Cat

- Proof that the kitten's pedigree has been registered
- Proof of transfer (the seller is furnished these forms by his association)
- A pedigree going back four generations
- A vaccination record

You should send these four items to the central office of your cat association, which, in return for a small fee, will send you a new pedigree valid in the United States.

Contract of Purchase

If you are buying a pedigreed cat, you should draw up a written agreement of purchase. Be sure to receive a written bill of sale and registration papers. Do not rely on verbal promises such as: "a kitten from the first litter will constitute payment," or "the cat can be sold back or given back if unsatisfactory," or "free stud service will be provided." Many friendships have been ruined by such vague promises. In any case, I would advise you to pay for your cat with cash rather than with services in kind.

Quite often the breeder will ask you to take the new kitten to your own veterinarian within two days of purchase. A legitimate breeder should also promise to let you return the new pet for a refund if it is not in good health.

Pedigree and Registry

Your written bill of sale should state the following:
- The above-mentioned privilege of return
- The date of purchase and any conditions of sale
- The price paid
- The registration numbers and names of both parents
- The litter or individual registration number of the kitten
- The kitten's date of birth and description (including breed, color, and sex)

With this bill of sale you should receive registration papers. If the breeder cannot supply those papers yet, be sure that this fact is indicated on the bill of sale, and that — as soon as the breeder receives these registration papers back from the registry (CFA or another body) — they will be sent to your immediately.

When kittens wrestle and fight in play, they are developing skills that take on a more serious form in later fights over territory.

Remember that you don't have to pay for the kitten's registration papers, as you have a right to them when purchasing your new kitten.

Along with these two papers, the breeder must supply written instructions on feeding and care, including dates of worming, medications used, etc., and a signed statement by a qualified veterinarian of all vaccinations given and information about future vaccinations.

The CFA (Cat Fanciers' Association) is the largest registry in the United States (and in the world). The ACA (American Cat Association) is very important too, and registers over 10,000 cats a year. Their addresses are on page 141.

Considerations Before You Get a Cat

How Old Should the Cat Be?

An ordinary kitten should be at least eight weeks old before it leaves its mother. Try to convince the owner to keep it up to that point. Unfortunately, kittens are sometimes given away at no more than four to five weeks old, and the new owner is then often forced to take the malnourished little creature, which may be suffering from chronic diarrhea as well, to the veterinarian for treatment. Even if you manage to save the cat's life at considerable expense and effort, it is likely to stay a runt all its life because of the deprivations suffered early on.

Breeders' regulations often stipulate that pedigreed cats not be separated from their mothers before they are twelve weeks old, but you should get acquainted with your kitten well before that time. The breeder from whom you are buying will surely let you visit a few times to see the kitten at different stages of development. This way you will quickly know whether it is healthy or not.

What a Healthy Kitten Looks Like

A healthy kitten is active, plays and runs around, wrestles with its siblings, looks a little clumsy but alert, eats its food with a good appetite, and purrs with happiness when nursing. It has clear, bright eyes without any trace of tearing, and its nose is cool and dry. It will be clean all over. Examine its rear end with special care: a healthy kitten produces solid feces; diarrhea leaves dirty traces on the fur. The ears should be clean and without dirt in the auricular cavity. If a young cat keeps scratching its ears or shaking its head constantly, this is probably an indication of mites (page 76).

Never buy a sick animal out of pity. If you do, you will have no end of trouble and expense, and you support irresponsible breeders to boot.

How to tell the sex of kittens. The distance between the anal and the genital apertures is longer in males (left) than in females (right); also, the sexual orifice is round in males and slit-like in females.

Telling the Sex

It is easiest to tell a kitten's sex when it is first born because the sex marks are not yet covered by fur. With an older kitten you have to wait until it is ten or twelve weeks old. At that point you can tell because the distance between the anus and the sexual orifice is larger in males than in females, and the orifice is round in males and slit-like in females.

14

Rules for Care

The Trip Home

A cat should be transported to its new home by car as quietly and calmly as possible and—whether the trip is a long or a short one—accompanied by two persons. You will find detailed instructions for trips and a description of cat carriers on page 31.

You will have asked the breeder in advance about your new charge's eating habits and have a can of its favorite food waiting for it. Everything will be ready for the arrival of the new member of the household.

Arrival in the New Home

When you get back home with the cat, you put the cat carrier down in the spot you have chosen in advance; you open the carrier and wait to see what happens. The kitten will soon get over the initial fear, peer out curiously, and then start exploring its new surroundings cautiously with slinky motions, usually along the walls. Often a kitten will find a hiding place under an armchair, sofa, or bureau. Never yank it out by force.

The kitten should be kept in one room for several days to get accustomed to its new surroundings before the door is left open for it to start exploring the rest of the apartment or house.

Going Outside

Your cat has to feel at home inside the house before you let it out, to the garden perhaps. Then give it an opportunity on a nice warm day to explore this new world bit by bit, but be sure to leave the door open. If the cat runs into anything scary, it will immediately dash back to the safety of home, and if the door is locked, will be out of luck. If you have a cat door (picture, page 15), your pet will be able to come and go as it pleases. Cat doors are available at pet stores; they are easy to install in any door and are burglarproof.

An intelligent cat can be taught to stay in a backyard or its immediate vicinity. But cats sometimes pay dearly for this freedom, particularly during mating season when they throw all caution to the winds and chase heedlessly after rivals and sexual partners. Some safety measures are therefore indicated. If you are enterprising and do not mind going to some expense, you can enclose your yard with wire mesh. The mesh can be stretched between tall, old trees along a boundary line, for instance. The fence should be at least 6 feet (2 m) high, preferably of wire with a green plastic coating, and bent inward at the top so that the cat is prevented from climbing over it. Tall trees near the fence that might provide routes of escape have to be made inaccessible with wire.

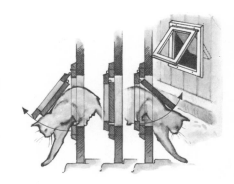

This is how cat doors function. They can be installed in any door and allow cats to come and go as they please.

Of course, if you live in a suburban development or in a community of row houses, your neighbors may object to looking out on what looks more like a bird cage than a garden.

Movement study I. Cats are agile climbers that can grab onto trees with their claws. When jumping off backwards, they twist in the air and land on the ground safely on all four feet.

For a cat that is cooped up inside an apartment all the time, a balcony can provide a needed change of scene. But to be entirely safe, it too has to be cat-proofed. If you live in a rented apartment, you should get your landlord's permission before you put up wire mesh. Do not ever think that your cat is too smart to jump from a balcony. I, too, had that illusion until a very intelligent cat of mine that had been happily sunning herself on the balcony for years suddenly leapt off it one day. Perhaps she had caught sight of a leaf gently floating downward or a bird flitting by. I shall never know. The cat survived the fall, but I could have spared her three weeks of discomfort while she recuperated if I had had the sense to enclose the balcony before the accident.

Open windows also represent a danger. You can prevent escape and falls quite easily by making sure all your windows are equipped with solid screens. Of course, screens are no protection against breaking and entering and are therefore insufficient for ground-floor apartments.

The Apartment Cat

The most important thing in the life of an apartment cat is its relationship to another being, whether another cat or a human cohabitant. Such a cat needs an extra large dose of affection and requires a lot of time for play and entertainment.

A cat that is kept exclusively indoors needs more than the basic minimum of equipment to live comfortably and contentedly. The list of necessary items includes food dishes, cat box, cat litter, a scratching post or tree, and a safe-feeling sleeping place like a basket or cardboard box. Toys are also needed for play with you and as a pastime when alone (page 22).

What a Cat Loves / What a Cat Hates

A Cat Loves	A Cat Hates
A place in the sun, by the stove, in the barn, on the sofa or a bed.	Rainy weather; being cold without a place to get warm.
Several play sessions with the cat's "own" person or with other cats every day.	A lonely life as an outcast or being isolated (for whatever reason).
Eating at the same time as the people and an occasional taste of human food.	Being fed carelessly and irregularly with food that is too hot or too cold or spoiled and served in dirty dishes.
Having a clean, dry litter box that is always accessible, even if the cat spends most of the time outside.	No litter box, or a dirty one; having to relieve itself outside no matter how bad the weather.
Nibbling on plants (perhaps until the plants die) because the tender shoots taste so good; throwing up on the rug afterwards.	Not being allowed to get near plants so there will be no chance of throwing up.
Gentle brushing and combing, but only when the cat feels like it.	Being combed when the cat has other things on its mind; pulling out lumps of matted hair. Cats also do not like to be petted vigorously the way dogs do.
Having clean, glossy fur.	Scaly skin; greasy, dull fur; ticks, fleas, and mites that cause itching.
A small number of planned litters in the case of a pedigreed cat; for an ordinary house cat, a soft life without kittens, stress, or danger.	Having kittens several times a year, which leaves a body pretty exhausted!
The quiet hum of friendly and low voices.	Noisy marital conflicts, children yelling, dogs barking, the din of cars and machinery, whining jet planes, firecrackers, and thunderstorms.
Visitors who make a fuss over the cat and perhaps bring a little present for it.	People who either ignore or, for whatever reason, detest the cat.
Catching a mouse now and then, chasing chickens, scaring birds, playing with little balls, crumpled paper, etc.	Being kept like a decorative object.
Sleeping undisturbed for hours at a time.	Having one's dreams of catching a mouse rudely interrupted and being shooed from one's sleeping place.
Balancing on top of tall pieces of furniture, weaving between glasses and vases, climbing up curtains, sharpening its claws on sofas and walls.	Being shut out of human habitations.

Rules for Care

The Cat on the Leash

If you want to take your cat for walks, you need a harness (picture below). Many cats refuse to enjoy this kind of fresh air exercise, although Siamese cats usually like it. Nonetheless, it is always a good idea to get a kitten used to wearing a harness. You can then let it lie on the back seat of the car on long trips, secured by a leash. Visits to the veterinarian's office are also easier if you can hold the cat by the leash.

For owners of apartment cats that are not allowed out, a harness and leash are a must for walks outside, visits to the veterinarian, and longer car trips.

Your Cat's House, Sleeping Place, or Basket

I would advise anyone who is about to get a cat — especially people who will not travel a lot with their cats — to get a carrier basket, which (with the gate removed and if you can succeed in rousting the cat out of your bed) will also serve as a sleeping place. This basket should be placed in a draft-free spot near a stove or radiator and then left undisturbed.

Most cats like caves or "houses" lined with plush or some other soft material. These can be bought ready-made at pet stores, but you can also build a perfectly adequate equivalent yourself. Take a square cardboard box and glue all sides and the top shut. Then cut one or more round openings about 8 inches (20 cm) in diameter. Pad the floor with a carpet sample or remnant and spread a piece of soft washable material over that. You can beautify the outside of the box by covering it with wall paper or carpeting — perhaps to match your decor — or with wrapping paper or decorative adhesive foil. The advantage of this home-made version is that it can be thrown out and replaced whenever it gets dirty, and whatever bacteria and germs might have accumulated in it end up on the dump.

The Litter Box

By the time kittens are ready to leave their first home, they are already house trained. Pet stores carry various models of litter boxes (picture, page 22). In my experience, a "house" type litter box with a removable tray at the bottom (similar to that of a bird cage) is the most satisfactory solution. Fill the tray with about 1 to 1½ inches (3 cm) of absorbent and deodorizing cat litter (cheaper if bought in large packages like twenty-five or fifty pound bags). There is no need to change the litter every day. Simply remove the wet places and feces with a slotted spoon or small trowel and fill in with fresh litter. The box should be washed once a week with hot water. Do not use strong disinfectants because cats do not

This wood pile in front of a window is a favorite ▷ hang-out for this housecat. Here she is sunning herself and meticulously grooming her coat.

like their smell and may look for another place to urinate.

Kittens under eight weeks old are too small to use the kind of box just described because the opening is too high. For them a plastic pan about 12 × 20 inches (30 × 50 cm) with a 2 inch (5 cm) rim is more suitable. Be sure the litter box is always accessible and easy to find. A good place for it is the bathroom, but then the bathroom door always has to be kept open.

Food and Water Dishes

My cats always have fresh water and dry food available. For this I use heavy, glazed ceramic bowls that cannot be pushed around or knocked over. I give them moist food, such as meat, canned food, and cooked cereals, in easy-to-clean and heatproof dishes. The food can be heated in them and served without dirtying other dishes, but please be careful not to put them down too hot.

◁ Above left: Friendship between a dog and a cat.
Above right: Peaceful coexistence of a rooster and a cat.
Middle left: This is how a mother cat carries her kitten which hangs rigidly from her mouth.
Middle right: This house cat is nursing her young in a pile of hay.
Below left: A cat drinking at a brook.
Below right: Meeting between two tomcats. The red tabby is trying a neutral approach with touching noses, and the gray tiger is taking on a threatening posture but retreating somewhat at the same time. In both cats, the hair on the back and tail is raised only moderately.

An artificial cat tree with a box at the top has to be both sturdy and stable because cats make use of it frequently and at length.

A Cat Rug or Cat Tree

Any cat, with or without pedigree, has a natural need to sharpen its claws. You therefore have to offer it something that is more tempting than upholstered furniture, which cats like to use for this purpose. Give your cat a rug, a piece of cardboard, or a post for scratching. For a cat that spends all its time indoors, a cat tree (pictured above) is ideal. All these items are available at pet shops for varying amounts of money. If you like to build things yourself, there are also cat trees you can assemble at home. If you design your own tree — start from scratch, so to speak — you have to watch out that it is properly balanced. A tree that falls over the first time a cat jumps on it is not likely to be used a second time. The best way to stabilize a cat tree is to secure it to the floor and ceiling with angle irons. My cats also like to sharpen their claws on scratching tubs I make for them myself. Take round, empty, plywood tubs and cover them inside and out with carpeting. The cats like to climb and race around on them and use them to sharpen their claws. Maybe you have other ideas; let your imagination run free.

Cat Toys

Pet stores and special cat boutiques have a whole array of cat toys for sale. Recently I saw an item that seems to me the ultimate in absurdity: a toy that simulates mouse catching. My own cats love playing with balls of crumpled newspaper and with old tennis and pingpong balls. They also like to chase after a rabbit's foot or a crocheted mouse, hide in newspapers stood up on end like A frames, or play hide and seek in clean, empty, cardboard boxes. Baskets of all shapes and sizes are also very popular.

Disinfectants

Be cautious when using disinfectants. Most of them contain phenol, which is highly poisonous to cats. Use a mild disinfectant, safe for cats (Rich Health, Mardel Laboratories, etc.). Ask your pet store for recommendations.

Care of the Coat

House Cats and Short-haired Cats

As a rule, ordinary house cats require no special grooming. They use their tongues to wash themselves several times a day and keep their fur shiny and free of dust. But my two

The ideal litter box (available at pet stores) has a drawer for the litter at the bottom; the hood over it protects the surrounding area from flying cat litter.

house cats love to be brushed. They are so eager that they keep pushing each other out of the way, each trying to get into my lap where I hold them for brushing. I consider some grooming important, especially at shedding time, and I work my cats over thoroughly with a brush and a rubber glove. I brush with my right hand, and I use my left one with a slightly moistened rubber glove to stroke them vigorously down the back. Try this procedure out on your cat once, and you will be surprised how much loose hair will come off, hair that the cat was not able to remove with its tongue. My cats purr ecstatically when I brush and stroke them, and every so often they roll over on their backs, probably to make sure I will not forget their bellies.

Brushing a cat is also a good opportunity to check for ticks and fleas. Cats that roam free pick up ticks not infrequently. These parasites can be removed by dabbing some baby or salad oil or some special tick liquid (available at pet stores) on them and carefully twisting

22

Rules for Care

them loose after a few minutes with tweezers or special tick pliers (also sold at pet stores). Be very careful not to leave the head in because this causes skin irritations (see also page 67). Fleas have to be combated vigorously because they are carriers of diseases and worm eggs. Your veterinarian will have a number of products for you to choose from: soaps, sticks, sprays, dips, and powders. When your cat is lying in your lap, purring and waiting to be brushed, you can also have a good look at its ears and check them for mites and dirt (treatment, page 76).

Long-haired Cats

Grooming a long-haired cat is much more time-consuming. Long-haired cats have to be combed thoroughly at least once a week. In the spring and fall, when the old fur is shed and a new coat grows in, daily combing is necessary to keep the fine hair of the undercoat from getting matted. You need two metal combs for this procedure (picture, page 25). Start with the coarser toothed comb, and then go over the whole cat again with the fine comb, paying special attention to the undercoat on the belly and between the legs.

Cats are naturally fastidious and lick the anal region carefully every day.

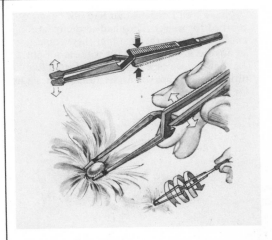

Implements for removing ticks properly. After the tick has been exposed in the fur, it is grabbed with tweezers or tick pliers and twisted very carefully until it can be pulled out of the skin.

Removing matted fur is not as difficult as people sometimes think. Fine hair mats more easily than coarser hair, and tight knots of fur are likely to form on the belly and between the legs. You will spot them quickly during the daily combing. Do not try to remove the entire knot all at once with the comb; separate it first into smaller parts with your fingers, and try to untangle these with the pointed handle of a comb. If this does not work, you can always cut the knot, but not with scissors, a regular knife, or a razor blade. Use a knife designed for opening seams that you can buy at a sewing center or a craft supply store. Guide the tip of this knife with your fingertip so that you will not accidentally cut the skin. These knives are very sharp, and the cat will hardly feel anything when you cut the knot out.

Rules for Care

I have seen Persians that had not been combed for weeks. They had so many hair knots so close to the skin that they would not let anyone get near their fur without a fight. Animals whose care has been neglected like this have to be shaved under full anesthesia by the veterinarian.

Long-haired cats have to be combed and brushed thoroughly every day if their fur is to maintain its glossy sheen.

You can use a fine louse comb even if your cat is free of pests; it will remove every last bit of dust from the fur.

The fur of a long-haired cat will retain its gloss and beauty if it is brushed every day with a brush with natural bristles. About once a month the cat should be cleaned with powder (ask your pet store) before the brushing, but apply the powder sparingly because it dries out the skin. It is best to let the powder work overnight and brush it out completely the next day. Black Persians should be bathed rather than powdered because the powder makes them look gray.

Siamese and Oriental Shorthairs

The fur of these cats should be short, shine like silk, and lie close to the body. All dead hairs therefore have to be removed. I use a brush with natural bristles and a slightly moist chamois cloth for this purpose. I use them simultaneously, running the cloth over the fur after each brush stroke. Daily grooming of this kind gets rid of all dead hairs and gives the coat the desired silky sheen. You can use a nubbly rubber brush instead, but you should never apply powder to an Oriental because it makes the fur stand out and look rough. Baths are also unnecessary for Orientals.

Care of the Eyes and Ears

Even the eyes of healthy house cats tear sometimes, or some dried discharge appears in the corners of the eyes. All you need to do is to wipe the eyes with a piece of cotton or a paper tissue dampened with some warm water. Always wipe in the direction away from the ear and toward the nose.

Typical Persians with a pronounced "stop" often suffer from a narrowing or plugging of the tear canals. This causes the eyes to tear, and the tears leave ugly yellowish stains on the fur. The tears have to be wiped off several times a day with a clean, soft, paper tissue. The veterinarian can also prescribe eye drops for your cat.

Check the ears of your cat regularly. Dirty ears can be cleaned carefully with a Q-tip dipped in water (see picture, page 76). If you repeatedly find dark little clumps of matter and the cat keeps scratching and shaking its head, consult the veterinarian because the discomfort might be caused by ear mites (page 76). In Persians, the ears sometimes look too large because of the tufts of hair at the tips of the ears. You can trim these tufts with rounded nail scissors. Remember this, particularly before you take your cat to an exhibition.

Rules for Care

Bathing — When and How?

As a general rule you should bathe a cat only if it is very dirty or if the treatment of a disease requires it. You can obtain good shampoos that are also effective against parasites from your veterinarian. Or you can use a baby shampoo or buy a shampoo at a pet shop.

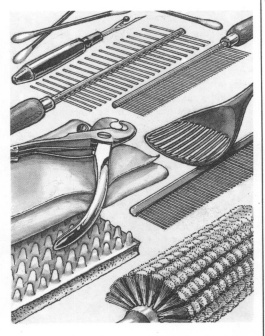

Utensils for grooming: cotton swabs for cleaning the ears (1); sewing blade for removing knots of fur (2); metal combs both wide and narrow-toothed (3 and 4); slotted spoon for cleaning out the cat box (5); toenail clippers (6); chamois cloth for shining the coat (7); fine-toothed comb of plastic or horn (8); rubber brush with nubbles (9); and brush with stiff bristles (10).

Bathe your cat in a well-heated room. Place it in a tub with lukewarm water (about 86°F [30°C]). Do not scare your cat by running or spraying water on it. Scoop up some water from the tub in your hand and pour it over the fur. The head should stay dry. After the bath you should rub the fur dry with a pre-warmed towel and let the cat dry completely in a warm room. Some cats do not object to the use of a hair dryer. If you want to exhibit your cat at a cat show, you should bathe it two or three days before the event. There are special "shampoos for pets" available for all hair colors of cats.

What to Do about Stud Tail

Not only sexually active tomcats but also castrated ones and even female cats may tend to have a greasy tail or "stud tail." In this condition, the gland on the upper side of the tail (supracaudal organ) secretes too much oil, which makes the tail look greasy and yellowish brown. Cleaning the affected area with alcohol for several days in a row controls the problem. Before you start this treatment, however, clip away the hair from the infected area. Since tail hair grows back only very slowly, you should not comb the tail or brush it too vigorously. You can also wash the tail in warm water with baby shampoo. Soap the fatty places well and brush them thoroughly with a soft toothbrush. Repeat this procedure until the tail is clean.

It is of course better not to let the tail get greasy. If you rub talcum powder into the tail hair down to the skin every week, let the powder work overnight, and blow it out thoroughly the next day, you will not have to worry about your cat getting a greasy tail.

Rules for Care

Care of the Claws

Cats that go outside take care of their claws themselves. They sharpen them on trees with obvious enjoyment. My house cats like best to use our young fruit trees for this purpose, which is why my husband has put scratching boards up around the tree trunks. I have also noticed that some of my cats like to "chew their nails."

Since Persians are often quite lazy in this respect, it is advisable to trim the claws on their front paws once or twice a year with special nippers (available at pet stores). Make sure you cut off only the tip of the claw, the part that does not have blood vessels. Watch your veterinarian perform this task a few times before you try it yourself. You should cut your cat's claws two days ahead of any cat show out of consideration for the judges.

Checking the Mouth and Teeth Regularly

Cats kept on a healthy diet should have perfect teeth. Unfortunately, both ordinary and pedigreed cats have a tendency to develop calculus and inflamed gums. This causes bad breath, excessive production of saliva, and difficulties in eating. Check the teeth of your cat regularly. If treatment is necessary you have to consult the veterinarian.

Start grooming the coat and checking the ears and teeth of your little cat early, when it is about twelve weeks old, so that it will get used to the routine. Most cats love to be brushed, particularly if you stop periodically to pet them.

Everyday Dangers

In the next few pages you will find listed some of the most frequent dangers to your cat's life and health as well as advice on how to minimize some of these risks by taking proper precautions.

How You Can Teach Your Cat

It is quite possible to teach a cat to respond to its name and to behave in certain ways. With some patient coaxing you may even teach your cat a few tricks. Apparently it depends more on the person than the animal whether a cat learns anything and develops into a pleasant member of the household or not.

The necessary prerequisites for success in such educational endeavors are: love for the animal, patience, consistency, authority, repetition, rewards, but never punishment. Only a person unfamiliar with cats and their ways would try to "teach the cat manners" in the sharp tone used for training dogs. But even such a person would soon realize that this approach not only does not work but actually upsets the animal, making it fearful or aggressive and thus totally unsuitable for a happy life with people.

Many a dog owner would be surprised and perhaps somewhat envious if he could see how my five cats that go in and out as they please come running from all directions as soon as I call their names. You can see that it is important to give your cat a name. Pedigreed cats usually come with a name, but this name is hardly ever used with the cat. You can give your ordinary house cat any name you please. Cats respond well to names ending with an "ee" sound, like Kitty, Pussy, etc. Whenever

List of Dangers

Source	Effects	Precautions
Cars	Being hit or run over.	Cannot be totally avoided; escape-proof your yard; training and neutering may reduce roaming.
Balcony	Danger of falling.	Enclose your balcony (nets are available at pet stores).
Iron	Burning nose when sniffing; pulling on cord and knocking iron down.	Do not leave cat alone in room with an iron.
Wire fences	Catching claws; the cat yanking at the wire and injuring itself.	Use fencing with soldered mesh.
Electrical wires	Chewing through wires, electric shock.	Pull all plugs before leaving apartment; otherwise watch cats carefully, especially young ones.
Windows	Escaping through an open window; falling from a great height; getting caught in a casement window (happens often!).	Install tough wire screening; never leave a casement window ajar.
Firecrackers	Fireworks can cause deafness or shock from fright if a device is set off too close to a cat; firecrackers can explode if a cat chews on them.	Do not set off fireworks; close windows and do not leave the cat alone on holidays when fireworks are displayed; stay with the cat and calm her.
Flea collar	Getting caught in bushes, branches, and fences (cat strangles).	Remove buckle and replace with a snap (check to see that it unsnaps).
Food	Food that is too hot or too cold or spoiled causes digestive problems; bones can get stuck in the throat.	Never give food directly from refrigerator; warm it to room temperature; remove bones or cook them until soft in a pressure cooker.
Broken glass	Cuts on paws and nose.	Sweep up broken glass promptly.
Rubber rings and erasers	Rubber is indigestible and stays in the stomach if eaten; rings can get caught around the neck.	Do not offer these items as toys or leave them lying around.

List of Dangers (continued)

Source	Effects	Precaution
Burners of a stove	Burning of the paws if the cat jumps on a hot burner.	Use covers on burners; do not leave cat alone in kitchen.
Dogs	Choking and biting by dogs; unfortunately, there are still dog owners who sic their dogs on cats.	Cannot be prevented with cats that roam free (see "Cars").
Other cats	Battles over territory and between toms result in torn ears and scratched faces.	Cannot be avoided with cats that are allowed outside, but the injuries are usually minor.
Candles	Knocking over the burning candle and danger of fire.	Do without candles.
Tinsel	The glitter tempts the cat to catch it; tinsel can be swallowed and is indigestible.	Do without tinsel.
Needles, pins	Can be swallowed; threaded needles are especially dangerous.	Be especially careful with sewing accessories and do not leave them lying around.
Oil, phenol	Contain substances toxic to cats; can be dangerous on contact.	This often cannot be avoided because cats like to sit under cars.
Plants	Injuries or poisoning.	Plants you should not have around: cacti, carnations, castor bean, Christ's-thorn, daphne, foxglove, horse chestnut, hyacinth, jimson weed, larkspur, laurel, lily-of-the-valley, lobelia, mistletoe, monkshood, narcissus, nightshade, poison hemlock, primrose, water hemlock and yew.
Plastic bags	Cats like to crawl into them, can get caught inside and suffocate.	Do not leave plastic bags lying around.
Rat poison	A cat may eat a mouse that was killed with poison (seldom fatal for cat).	Do not use rat poison yourself and convince neighbors that cats are effective, biological pest control agents and were used by the ancient Egyptians to keep granaries rodent-free.

List of Dangers (continued)

Source	Effects	Precaution
Cupboards	Kittens can get caught behind or underneath them or climb up too high and get hurt jumping down.	Keep young kittens (up to twelve weeks old) with their mother in a hazard-free room where they were born; later only prudence and careful watching help.
Drawers	Cats like to crawl into and hide in dark, cave-like places and may be forgotten in a closed drawer.	Check before closing a drawer to make sure no cat is hiding there.
Toys	Children's toys made of plastic may be chewed on or swallowed (indigestible).	Urge children to pick up after playing.
Hot plates	Burns, knocking over, danger of fire.	Electric plate warmers are less dangerous.
Electric outlets	Nose gets too close, danger of electric shock.	Use safety covers.
Chairs	Paws can get caught in ornamental decorations of wooden and wrought-iron chairs.	This does not happen with plain chairs.
Tablecloths	Catching a claw when reaching up from the floor, pulling tablecloth down, and being burnt by hot soup or coffee.	Place mats do not stick out over the edge of the table and cannot be pulled down.
Doors	Getting caught in them; being locked in or out.	Only careful watching can prevent escape and accidents.
Parasites	Fleas, mites, ticks, and worms can be disease carriers.	Check your pet regularly.
Washing machine	Accidentally locking the cat in front-loading machines.	Caution: never leave the door open; check by reaching in before each use.
Detergents, cleaning agents, chemicals	Poisoning; acid burns from licking or accidental contact.	Keep all household cleansers locked away in cupboards.
Yarn	Wrapping yarn around paws and neck.	Do not offer balls of yarn for playing; suspend toys about 4 inches above the ground on a thread tied to the back of a chair.
Cigarettes	Burns; nicotine poisoning from eating the tobacco.	Best to give up smoking; otherwise use ash trays with covers.

you pet or feed your cat, talk to her and say her name, especially at the beginning. She will then soon associate everything pleasant, like eating and getting petted or brushed, with this name, and when you call her name, she will appear quickly. If she is in some place you do not want her to be, do not scold her and use her name but scare her away with a "shoo" or say a loud and clear "No, no!" as I do.

Teaching a cat tricks requires time and patience on your part but is probably quite a lot of fun for the cat. Practice daily, but not too long. When you see any sign of the cat losing interest, stop the practice session.

Sit up and beg. Hold a tidbit in front of the sitting cat's nose and raise it slowly until the cat rises up. Wait until she sits on her haunches and then give it to her as a reward while saying "Up!" Repeat this game, but only as long as the cat enjoys it.

Fetch. My Siamese cat Anima fetches things without my having taught her. I think she does this not out of obedience but in response to a natural instinct that makes animals bring prey back to the nest for their young. Anima retrieves fur mice, rabbits' feet, and all kinds of toys, returning them to me in big leaps. Then she sits and waits with intense attention for me to throw the object again. Most cats love this game. But make sure the object is neither too small nor too large — mouse size is ideal — and that its smell appeals to the cat's nose.

Talk. When I ask my Birman "Who is the best cat in the world?" she always responds with a "meow." Often one can teach a cat to "talk" by holding a bit of food in front of her nose, raising it, and asking "Who wants something to eat?" Usually she will look at the food with interest and say "Meow, meeow, mee." It is up to you to find the right tone and questions that will prompt the cat to "answer." Once she has caught on, you can keep asking her questions. Just make sure, when you are showing her off before friends, that you ask questions that should be answered with a "Me!"

Be sure to praise your cat after every little trick, even if the performance was not quite perfect. Show your appreciation by talking to her and giving her a special goody.

Traveling with Your Cat

Even the most ordinary of cats will have to be taken somewhere sometime during its life, if only to the veterinarian's for shots.

A female pedigreed cat usually travels to visit a stud since a stud of the desired quality is usually not found just around the corner. Many cats are also shown at exhibits and sometimes have to travel considerable distances. There are also pet lovers who do not want to leave their cats behind and take them along on vacation trips. I have a friend in Stockholm who takes her three Rex cats along to her country house every weekend. The cats look forward to these excursions as much as she does: after a week in a city apartment, they appreciate being able to roam around outside without restraints.

What is important is that the cats be transported safely whether in a car, on a train, or by air.

Car and Train Trips

A cat lying on the shelf by the rear window of a car may look decorative, but this way of traveling is dangerous. The cat could easily cause an accident by leaping on the neck of the driver or crawling around on the floor near the brake and gas pedals. Or in case of an accident, the car door could be opened and, in all the excitement, be left standing

Rules for Care

open. The cat escapes. Upset by the strange surroundings, she may run away even from people she knows. Because of these possibilities, a cat in a car should always be restrained either by being placed in a carrier or by wearing a harness that is secured to the back seat.

A carrier should be large enough so the cat can stand up, turn around, and lie down stretched at full length. Shipping crates for air transport meet these requirements best. They also have ventilation grates and escape-proof doors and are therefore the safest and most comfortable travel containers for cats. Mark your home address and phone number and the vacation address on the container.

The bottom of the carrier should be padded with a thick layer of newspapers for warmth and to absorb urine.

A sleeping basket (right) that can be closed is all that is necessary for short trips as, for instance, the trip to the veterinarian. Not suitable for transporting cats are small baskets or cardboard boxes, shopping baskets or bags, or rabbit and hamster cages. I also do not think pillow cases are ideal, even though people occasionally carry their cats in them when they bring them to our practice. In a pinch, of course, a pillow case is better than carrying a very nervous cat on your arm without a leash.

Among cats, just as among people, there are active sight-seers who love to ride in a car and who watch the world go by with interest, and there are more phlegmatic types who sleep away the whole trip. Still others hate to be cooped up and complain pitiably for hours on end. There are even cats that suffer from travel sickness and vomit when they have to travel by car. (You can get tablets [Bonine®] for this from your local pet store, or a medication prescribed by a veterinarian.)

You should in any case get your cat used to traveling by car when it is young. Start with short trips, and talk to the cat in a calming

This sleeping basket with a gate that can be locked doubles as a transport container. The cat will feel safe and content in its familiar basket on car trips and on the way to the veterinarian.

voice. But do not let it out of its carrier no matter how pathetically it complains. The danger of unpredictable behavior out of fear is too great. You can gradually increase the length of the trips until the cat gets used to the sounds of a car and to this different situation. If a cat will simply not adjust to car travel, the veterinarian can prescribe a tranquilizing medication that can be put in the cat's food before a trip.

If you leave your cat in the car in summertime, make sure the car is parked in the shade. Otherwise the cat might suffer a heatstroke. You should also leave two windows cracked so that the air inside the car can circulate.

Tips for traveling with a cat: Feed the cat for the last time before the trip six to eight hours before leaving. Your cat can drink as

31

late as two or three hours before the departure. Do not give it food or drink on the trip.

In the United States you can usually take your cat along on the train without paying extra. The cat has to travel in a carrier and must not be removed from it during the trip. Of course, the cat is not entitled to a seat, and, out of consideration for other passengers, should be transported as unobtrusively as possible in a completely enclosed container because there are people who do not like cats and are even afraid of them.

Travel on buses and trains of most urban transportation systems is also free. Here, too, the cat should be in an enclosed container. Your cat will feel more secure if it can watch the throng of people from the safety of its little "house." Try to avoid traveling with your pet on buses, streetcars, and subways during the rush hours before 9 A.M. and after 4 P.M. because of the crowded conditions and because the bustle will make your cat even more nervous than it already is.

Trips by Air

If you plan to fly with your cat, you should inquire at the airline of your choice what the regulations are because each company handles the question differently. If you tell the airline in advance that you will have a cat with you, and if there is no dog on the plane, you may be able to take your cat with you in the passenger cabin. In that case the carrier must be of a size that fits under the seat. One time I flew to a cat show in Paris carrying a young Birman in a travel bag for cats and holding her in the lap the whole time. On short flights that last no more than one or two hours this is quite feasible.

If you have ordered a pedigreed cat from England or Europe or some other part of the world, it is unlikely that you will pick up the animal yourself. You will probably have it sent instead. You can leave the transport up to the airline without worrying. The animals travel in comfortable containers in a pressurized section of the plane. Of course, you have to pick your cat up promptly at the airport.

Travel Abroad

A rabies vaccination (page 64) is required for all travel abroad and is necessary for re-entry into the United States. I only take cats abroad that have comprehensive vaccination protection: that have had shots against rabies, distemper, and upper respiratory infections.

An official health certification should, as a rule, be no older than five days and sometimes has to be translated into the language of the country in question and notarized by the consulate. Very often this procedure is extremely complicated and time-consuming, as I found out one time when my little male Birman traveled to Brazil. That is why I strongly advise you to inquire well ahead of time at the local office of the United States Department of Agriculture where you will be guided to the right channels.

Staying Overnight at a Hotel

First of all you have to inquire whether or not the hotel of your choice accepts guests with pets. If you are traveling with an unneutered tomcat, you should choose a hotel room with a large bathroom because a room where a male cat has sprayed beds and curtains cannot be rented again for several days. The tomcat has to spend the entire stay in the bathroom, which you can make more homelike with a comfortable bed or basket and blanket. Only hotels that have had bad experiences with pets and their owners refuse to accept people traveling with animals.

The Proper Way of Dealing with a Cat

What to do if the cat...	Wrong	Right
Steals some meat.	Take away the booty; punish the animal.	Do not leave any food around; always feed the cat in the same place.
Scratches wallpaper or sofa.	Yell at it and chase it away.	Carry it gently to the cat tree and show it — with your fingernails — how to use the tree.
Wanders.	Scold it upon its return and lock it out as punishment.	Greet it warmly and make an appointment for neutering at the vet's. (Neutered cats, both male and female, hardly roam at all.)
Misses the cat box.	Dunk its nose in the puddle.	Clean the box more frequently but without using disinfecting agents; set up additional litter boxes, especially in the cat's chosen urinating spots; use larger litter boxes.
Begs at table.	Chase it away, lock it out.	If you feed your cat or give it a goody at mealtimes, it will stop begging.
Sprays against walls and furniture.	Put up new wallpaper, berate the cat.	Put an end to these markings by having the cat neutered.
Wants to get off your lap or out of your arms.	Tighten your grip; this will make the cat put up a fight.	Loosen your hold, put the cat down, pick it up again, and talk to it gently to distract it.
Scratches or bites in the course of play.	Scratch or bite back; pull your hand away.	Keep your hand still, talk to the cat gently, and pet it with your other hand.
Sleeps in your bed.	Here there is no agreement among experts. If you live alone, you can let your cat have its way. If you do not live alone and your partner refuses to share his or her pillow with a cat, get your cat a companion (both animals can be of the same sex).	

Nutrition of Cats

Although cats have been domesticated for thousands of years, they are still predators by nature. In order to stay healthy, they need not only meat but also small amounts of vegetable matter and minerals, both of which are present in concentrated form in the intestines of the prey a wild cat would eat.

Domestic cats that have gone wild usually live on scraps and on the mice they hunt. This is generally all they need to live on. Contrary to what people often think, even house cats that are fed regularly also catch mice. My two neutered Siamese and my two ordinary house cats keep our house and barn free of mice and rats even though their dishes are filled twice every day. Cats catch mice not just to satisfy hunger but also because of a strong hunting instinct. Quite often they chase prey not for eating but for depositing as a present on the door mat.

Eating Habits of Cats

From the way a cat eats — not only an ordinary house cat but also a pedigreed cat that has never set eyes on a mouse, let alone caught and eaten one — you can tell that it is a beast of prey. If you feed a cat a piece of meat the size of a mouse, the cat will not eat it right away unless very hungry but instead will shake it, pull it off the plate, throw it up in the air, gulp it down without chewing, then regurgitate it, and sometimes hide it. Even very young kittens will defend their "prey" against siblings by growling and spitting. Liquid or mushy food, on the other hand, does not evoke this response, and several cats will eat together from one dish without any show of antagonism.

Natural Food (Prey)

Mice rank first on the menu of any cat's preferred foods. That is why cats will spend the best part of their day catching mice if there are any mice to be caught where they live. Because of their strong hunting instinct, they will kill shrews and moles as well, although they do not eat them afterwards. Although small animals (mice, birds, chicks) are a cat's natural food, they can carry parasites and harmful bacteria, as can scraps of raw meat from the butcher's. And hardly any cat owner will be able to supply freshly killed prey to a cat that is entirely dependent on humans for its food.

Foods You Can Prepare Yourself

There are elaborate feeding charts for cats that list scientifically calculated amounts of needed food values and vitamins and that provide menu plans for the whole week. But you can also feed your cat much more simply with foods you prepare yourself.

Like most cat owners I give my cats a homemade meal every now and then instead of the usual commercial food.

Muscle meat. Muscle meat from all kinds of meat animals is the most important source of proteins for cats, and various innards provide a change in diet and supply certain vitamins.

When you buy meat for your cat you will want to consider not only how nutritious it is and how it agrees with the cat but also how much it costs. Cheaper cuts that are somewhat fatty and sinewy and organ meats in reasonable proportions are quite adequate for cats.

Depending on what is available, you can feed your cat raw beef or meat from horses, rabbits, chickens, and turkeys (heart and tripe are particularly cheap). Pork, including organ meats from pigs, has to be well cooked because it can carry diseases like toxoplasmosis and Aujeszky's disease (page 79).

Liver. Liver is an important source of energy and vitamins (especially vitamin A). When it is fed raw it can cause diarrhea, and when cooked it can have the opposite effect on the intestines. Do not give your cat too much liver or only liver because this might cause vitamin A poisoning under certain circumstances.

Kidneys. Kidneys, especially beef kidneys, are quite cheap and can occasionally be fed to cats. It is a good idea to soak them in cold water first.

Heart. Besides heart being very nutritious, most cats like to eat it.

Lung. Very cheap and sometimes available at no cost, lung sounds attractive, but it is relatively low in food value and most cats are not very fond of it. Lung has to be cut up into small pieces or pureed.

Cows' udders. The same is true of cows' udders, and they sometimes carry the disease agents that cause mastitis in cows.

Spleen. Consisting mostly of membranous tissue and blood, spleen has a purgative effect similar to that of raw liver.

Tripe. Although tripe is an excellent food for dogs, it is less suitable for cats because it is so tough.

If you give your cat a large piece of meat now and then, it gives the cat a chance to exercise its chewing muscles. The pieces should be about the size of plums or of mice. About one quarter to one half pound (120 to 250 grams) per day is plenty.

Bones. Bones are good for cats because they supply necessary minerals (cats eat their prey whole, including the skeleton). But bones from large animals are impossible for cats to eat, and poultry bones, especially after they are cooked, are dangerous because they are splintery and sharp and can get stuck in the mouth, between the teeth, or in the throat. Bones of young animals, cooked until soft in a pressure cooker, can be included in a cat's diet, but generally you will have to resort to bone meal and mineral supplements to cover your cat's need for minerals.

Fish. Most cats like a fish day now and then. Some frozen fish fillets are relatively cheap. They should be cooked and deboned before being fed to a cat. Cats that eat fish sometimes smell a little fishy themselves.

If a cat is a very close member of the household it is almost impossible not to give it tidbits from the table occasionally. Cats seem to appreciate this as a gesture of affection. Morsels of food that people at the table are eating are consumed by cats with evident enjoyment even though the cats would spurn such food served in their own dishes. There is nothing harmful to the cat's health about feeding it an occasional bit of mashed potato, noodles, pudding, or vegetable.

Margarine. Cats also like to lick vitamin-enriched margarine off your finger now and then, and this aids their digestion.

Egg yolk. You can give your cat a raw egg yolk two or three times a week. (Raw white of egg contains avitin which destroys B vitamins in the food.) You can also add small amounts — about one ounce (20 to 30 grams) — of vegetables and starchy foods like potatoes, rice, noodles, or oatmeal to your cat's food occasionally. Here it is a good idea to mix all the food together so the cat does not simply pick out the pieces of meat.

My cats also like oatmeal made with three tablespoons of instant oat cereal for infants, one teaspoon food yeast, one egg yolk, and one cup of warm milk (but without sugar!). Watch your cat's stool because milk can cause diarrhea (page 72).

Nutrition of Cats

If you do feed your cat food you have prepared yourself you should add yeast flakes (about one teaspoon per day) and vitamin and mineral supplements.

Commercial Food

Canned Food

Canned cat food is ideal. It is always ready to use, can be stored, is easy to take along on trips, and contains all the necessary vitamins, minerals, and trace elements.

Canned cat food is a complete food, so it contains everything a cat needs to eat to stay healthy. There are many brands on the market. Read the nutritional information on the label carefully. Most products sold are a well-balanced combination of nutrients especially designed to meet the needs of cats. Canned cat food comes in a number of different flavors such as beef, chicken, or fish.

Canned cat foods contain not only meat (red meat, heart, liver, lung) but also grains (rice, barley, wheat, corn) and vegetables and food yeast. The proportions of protein, fat, carbohydrates, vitamins, and trace elements are very similar to those found in the natural prey of cats.

Cats that are fed tidbits from the table will help themselves if you turn your back.

For the treatment of urolithiasis (page 77), special canned foods are available that can be given as part of a "kidney stone diet" prescribed by your veterinarian.

Dry Food

Dry food is also a complete food and available in different flavors. The difference between it and canned food is that it contains less water (canned food has 75 percent, dry food only 15 percent). That is why it is important that a cat that is fed dry food always have fresh water available. Dry food is more concentrated and has more food value than canned food, and your cat does not need to eat as much of it to cover its energy needs.

Each cat should have its own food and water dishes. If a whole cat family has to eat from one dish, young kittens in particular get less than their fair share.

Kittens—favorite pets of children.
Above: Persian kittens, blue-cream, red, and red and white. ▷
Middle: House cat with tiger markings and with white patches.
Below: Young house cat and young Birman Sealpoint.

Nutrition of Cats

Grass

Every cat likes to nibble occasionally on something green. There are several plants your cat should stay away from, but there are also some that are good for it. Umbrella plants *(Cyperus alternifolius)* are in this latter category. If you live in a city apartment, you may want to buy a little box of soil seeded with this grass at a pet store. If you decide to plant some grass, oats, wheat, or other greens in a pot or window box yourself, be sure you do not use any pesticides. In the summer you can simply pick some young grass in a clean meadow (not along a road). Grass is particularly important for Persians. Usually cats vomit after eating grass. This is how they get rid of hairs they have swallowed while licking themselves clean. My Birman likes any kind of green leaves. If I don't give her any, she takes whatever she can find. I often find balls of fur she has vomited, especially when she is shedding.

Water and milk

The proper drink for cats is water, which should always be available to them. Replace the water every day and offer it in a freshly washed dish. If you feed your cat dry food, it is especially important that the cat always have access to enough liquid. Many cats prefer to drink water that has sat for a while like the water in puddles, in aquariums, and in flower vases. As long as the cat also has fresh water available, this is nothing to worry about. Some cats also enjoy catching drops of water from a faucet.

Milk, which is an excellent source of protein and calcium, is especially important for nursing mother cats. You can give your cat milk fresh from the cow or bottled milk. It should not, however, be low fat milk or milk diluted with water because cat's milk is much richer in fats and proteins that cow's milk. Canned milk can be thinned with one-third water. Young kittens also like cereal mixed with milk.

There are many cats that drink milk without adverse effects, but in others milk causes diarrhea. By adding or withholding milk you can regulate your cat's digestion as necessary (in case of constipation, give milk; in case of diarrhea, withhold it). The laxative effect of milk is the result of the lactose in it. Since the lactose is used up in the process of souring, milk products like yogurt and cottage cheese do not cause diarrhea.

Feeding Times

Cats have no regular eating schedule in nature. They can occasionally go without food for considerable periods and then make up for it with a huge meal. But the organism of a cat is basically geared to hunting and several feedings a day. Get your cat used to regular mealtimes and uniform amounts of food. This is the only way you can check on its appetite. Even a cat used to living outdoors will quickly adjust to a set feeding routine and will turn up at the right time when it is hungry. A kitten should be fed two to four times a day, a grown cat once or twice (table, page 42). The food should be at room temperature, never hot or cold. Please do not leave the leftover food standing around but put it in the refrigerator or throw it out.

◁ Young Siamese playing with a ball. These pictures clearly show this breed's amazingly quick reactions and talent for jumping.

Nutrition of Cats

When drinking, a cat curls its tongue backwards and then ladles milk or water into the mouth.

Amount of Food

As far as the amount and kind of food are concerned, there is no difference between pedigreed and ordinary cats. Both eat what they need and as much as their appetite dictates. Of course, there are cat owners who spoil their pets with steak, ham, and chicken. Cats who are fed like this then refuse other, healthier diets and consequently often suffer from deficiencies and digestive problems. Because of a long process of natural selection, sometimes under harsh conditions, there are ordinary cats that are less fussy about their food than many pedigreed cats. When you plan your cat's menu you do not have to stick to the given amounts of calories meticulously but simply use them as guidelines. Start your newly acquired kitten out on only about three tablespoons of the canned food the breeder recommended and observe how much of it is eaten. If there is some left over, give a little less next time. If everything is cleaned up, offer a little more. You will soon learn just how much food your cat needs. Cats that spend a lot of time outdoors are hungrier than cats that stay inside. Male cats eat more than females, and neutered animals tend to put on weight and should be fed sparingly. The food of pregnant cats should be increased somewhat and given in three or four smaller meals a day. Give a nursing cat plenty of food and let her eat as much of it as she needs (table, page 42). Cats are individualists in eating as in everything else. Cats of mine that are of the same age and weigh the same consume entirely different amounts of the same food.

How to Avoid Mistakes in Feeding

Make sure the food is varied. Breeders of cats have to prevent young kittens from getting used to just one kind of food (only raw beef, heart, liver, or fish). Of course, it is also possible to turn a grown cat into a fussy eater, and it is extremely difficult to change the eating habits of such a spoiled cat and get it to accept a less expensive and healthier diet. You have to proceed with much patience and perseverance, mixing in with its favorite menu first a little bit, and then gradually more, of what you think the cat should eat.

Dog owners who have just acquired a cat often ask me whether they can feed the cat dog food. Generally speaking, this should not be done because dog food is designed for dogs and contains considerably less protein than cat food. If the cat lives on nothing but dog food, it will therefore not get enough protein. But if one day there is only dog food in the house, it will do the cat no harm to eat that for a change.

Do not overfeed your cat! This is especially easy to do with apartment cats that are neutered. Since the relationship between these animals and their people is often very close and these cats are especially good at begging,

Nutrition of Cats

Movement study II. These four drawings show how a cat stretches its spine and joints when it gets up from a rest.

it is hard to resist them. But firmness is essential for their physical well-being.

It is not enough to give cats that go out to hunt only milk and a few scraps. Do not assume that there are always enough mice around for the cat to be essentially self-sufficient.

Never feed raw pork because of the diseases it can cause (page 79).

The food should be neither too cold nor too hot. About 80°F (28°C) suits the body temperature of a cat.

Do not give your cat table scraps like bones and cartilage. But you can give it other scraps it likes without hesitation. Just make sure the food is not too salty or spicy and does not contain sugar.

Please do not be haphazard about when you feed your cat (page 39).

The most common mistake is that cats are not fed enough protein. Good, protein-rich foods for cats are mother's milk (let the kittens nurse as long as possible), red meat, innards, poultry, fish, cheese, milk, cottage cheese, egg yolk, and soy bean, corn, and barley flakes.

Do not puree all the cat's food. Pureeing or blending is advisable only for sick cats or old, toothless ones, or if you are trying to change the food habits of a spoiled cat by mixing in less popular items.

If you have more than one cat, each should have its own dish. Do not feed a whole cat family from one dish. Young cats in particular should be given separate dishes because otherwise some will always get less than their share.

Since cats like to leave a little bit of food in their dish and this food spoils quickly, especially in warm weather, you have to throw out old food and wash the dishes regularly.

Many cats lose their appetite when they are not fed by "their" person or if food is offered to them in a strange dish or unfamiliar place. Keep in mind: same person, same dish, same location for feeding. It is also a good idea to feed your cat at the same time that you eat. This does not mean, of course, that it has to sit at the table with you (though this does happen).

Feeding Plans

The following table is meant as a guideline for feeding your cat.

| **All-purpose food per day (canned)** | | | | |
Age	Feedings per day	Amount per day (in grams)	kcal*	kJ*
Kittens 7–12 weeks	4	90	90	380
Half-grown cats 3 lb (1.5 kg)	2	140	140	590
Grown cats ca. 9 lb (4 kg)	1–2	340	340	1430
Old cats (over 10 years)	3–4	200	200	840
Pregnant cats	1–2	360	360	1510
Nursing cats	3–4	450	450	1890
Active studs	1–2	400	400	1680
Neutered cats	1	250	250	1050

* kcal = kilocalorie; kJ = kilojoule;
1 kcal = 4.2 kJ. One gram of all-purpose cat food contains about 1 kcal.

A Cat's Body and What It Can Do

Basic Anatomy

Cats are mammals. Like all living creatures, they are made up of cells, which are differentiated to form various structures and organs. The cells are the basic building blocks of a complex organism with a definite structure and form, capable of performing the varied life processes.

The moving apparatus is formed by the skeleton and the musculature. A highly developed nervous system (consisting of a brain, a spinal cord from which nerve bundles branch off, and sensitive nerve endings in the various organs) directs the functioning of the body, takes in external stimuli, and coordinates movements.

Vitally necessary oxygen is absorbed by the lungs and carried by the blood, which is propelled by the heart through the circulatory system to all the parts of the body.

The stomach and digestive tract, together with the closely associated pancreas and liver, break down the food and thus supply the body with the elements necessary for maintaining body tissue and with the energy for functioning.

The kidneys rid the circulating blood of the poisonous waste products of metabolism and eliminate them, together with excess salts, through the urinary tract.

The body is covered all over with a skin that protects the organism against harmful external influences. The skin can also secrete sweat and thus regulates the balance of fluids and body temperature.

Hormones, in coordination with the nervous system, direct and time the course of many body functions. And a complex defense system of specialized blood and tissue cells helps the organism reject foreign substances and fight pathogens (viruses and bacteria)

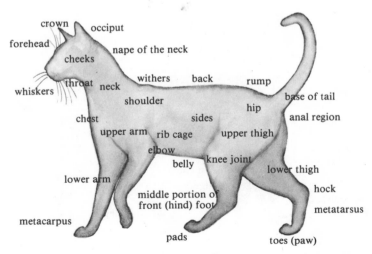

What is what on a cat? Knowing the names of the various parts of a cat's body is helpful, especially when talking to the veterinarian.

A Cat's Body and What It Can Do

as well as parasites. The sexual organs have the function of maintaining the species.

Specialized Hunting Functions

The shape and structure of an animal always reflect the demands made on it by its specific way of life: they reflect the animal's needs, its behavior, and its capacities. The body of a cat is the result of evolution, and it displays the perfected qualities of a hunter of small, fast-moving prey. Its excellent senses allow a cat to spot prey at a distance and to go after it instantly and skillfully. A powerful and supple body, great speed and jumping ability, strong teeth, and mobile paws equipped with sharp claws enable a cat to kill prey quickly and effectively once it is caught.

Skeleton and Musculature

The skeleton gives an animal its basic shape and protects the delicate internal organs from external injuries. Its structure allows the muscles and tendons to move the individual bones in their joints in such a way that all the necessary movements can be performed at a minimum expense of energy. An effective lever system in the hind parts together with strong muscles in the back give the cat its great jumping power and amazing speed. This speed can be maintained only over short distances, however; cats are not capable of record performances in long-distance running.

Another trait worth mentioning here is that cats can rotate their forelimbs to a much greater degree than humans or anthropoids can. The construction of their shoulder joints

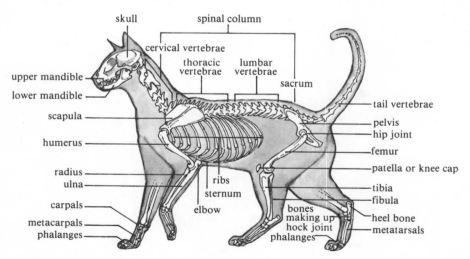

Structure of the body and skeleton: The most important features of a cat's skeleton are the exceptionally supple spine and the arrangement of the leg bones to which strong muscles are attached.

A Cat's Body and What It Can Do

is such that they can turn their front paws inward and hold on firmly to prey or grab on to a tree to climb it.

Paws and Claws

Cats are digitigrade: they walk on their toes. Their paws correspond to the toes and fingers in humans. They have five toes on the front paws and four on the hind feet. The claws on the hind feet are usually worn down by walking, but the claws on the front remain sharp as needles because they are retracted when the cat walks.

The amazing general suppleness and elasticity of the moving apparatus, together with soft pads on the feet, allow cats to move silently.

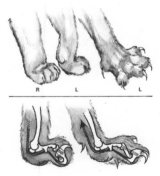

When a cat walks or runs, the claws of the front paws are retracted into their skin pockets and are therefore always needle-sharp.

Teeth and Digestive Tract

A cat has thirty teeth. The most obvious ones are the large, slightly curved, cuneiform canines with which a cat can grab its prey securely and kill it. The molars work like scissors and cut the prey up into bite-size pieces. Cats are basically meat eaters, and their mouths are adapted to that kind of food. They cannot move their jaws sideways very well, and are therefore unable to grind or chew their food with their mouths closed and lather it with saliva. That is why they always chew on large prey with the side of the mouth, cutting off large pieces of it and swallowing them whole.

The deciduous, or baby, incisors are grown to full size at about eight weeks, and at five to six months they are replaced by the permanent ones. The entire set of permanent teeth is complete at seven to nine months.

$$\text{Upper Jaw} \quad \frac{1\ 3\ 1\ 3 \qquad 3\ 1\ 3\ 1}{1\ 2\ 1\ 3 \qquad 3\ 1\ 2\ 1} = 30\,\text{teeth}$$
$$\text{Lower Jaw}$$

Cats have six incisor teeth each in the upper and lower jaw. Each jaw also has two canines, and the upper jaw has eight molars, the lower, six. That makes a total of sixteen teeth above and fourteen below.

The cat's rough tongue is covered with spinelike projections and has the function of getting meat off the bones when the cat is consuming a prey animal. It also serves as an excellent tool for grooming. When kittens are first born, they have a rim of spines along the edge of their tongues. These spines serve to hold onto the mother's teats, which the little tongues encircle like pipes.

The gastric juices of cats not only digest unchewed pieces of food but also break down bones and destroy bacteria contained in the

A Cat's Body and What It Can Do

food. That is why cats are relatively immune to diseases passed on in food.

In the relatively short intestine, the food which has been broken down by gastric acid and enzymes is reabsorbed, and enters the blood stream. One fact worth noting is that the intestines of domestic cats are somewhat longer than those of their wild cousins. This difference is probably the result of long domestication during which cats led quieter lives and ate food that contained more roughage and carbohydrates than their natural diet. In the large intestine, most of the fluid is extracted from the waste matter, which is then formed into firm feces.

The entire digestive process, from the time when food is eaten until it is eliminated as feces, takes about twenty-four hours. The active metabolism of a little cat calls for frequent nourishment in small doses, supplied in nature by small prey animals. The cat always has to be in top shape so it will be able to react quickly, will be ready to jump at any moment, and will be fit for hunting. A full belly and layers of fat will not do for this kind of life.

The Coat

A cat's coat protects the body against changes in the environment. It shields the animal against cold and wet. A cat that lives outdoors and is sufficiently well nourished adapts the thickness of its undercoat to the temperature fluctuations of the seasons so well that it will not be cold even in below-freezing weather. This assumes, of course, that the animal has a dry place to retreat to. A cat used to living indoors, on the other hand, would suffer greatly from the cold if it were suddenly forced to live outside in wintertime.

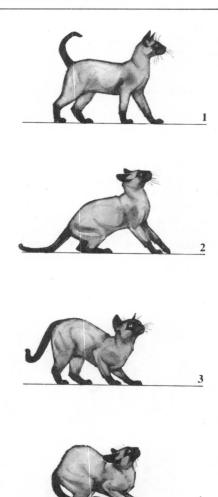

Movement study III. Postures expressing different moods: self-assured and attentive (1); uncertain and pulling back (2); retreating but ready for defense (3); fear and readiness to fight (4).

A Cat's Body and What It Can Do

The Tail

A cat uses its tail both to maintain its balance when jumping or falling and to express different moods. But cats get along quite well, too, with only a stub of a tail or no tail at all if they lose it in an accident.

Sexual Organs

The reproductive cells that pass on the genetic heritage to future generations (pages 96–97) are formed in the ovaries of the female cat and in the testes of the male. These organs also produce sex hormones that determine the different anatomical sex characteristics and sexual behavior of the cats (pages 85–86). Depending on their breed and state of nourishment, young cats reach sexual maturity at seven to twelve months. It is often difficult to tell the sex of a young kitten by external characteristics (picture, page 14). The sexuality of cats, particularly of tomcats, and their prolific nature present responsible cat owners with a problem that they usually solve by neutering their pets (page 83).

The sexual organs of a female cat consist of two bean-shaped ovaries that are about 1/4 inch (7 mm) long and 1/8 inch (4 mm) thick. They are located in the abdominal cavity on either side of the spinal column behind the kidneys and near the tips of the uterine horns. The uterus divides just above the cervix into two long "horns" in which the developing embryos are lined up in a row in a pregnant cat. The placenta, which is connected by blood vessels to the walls of the uterus, provides all the nourishment the fetuses need until they are born. The placenta surrounds each fetus like a belt. Right after birth, these hose-like formations are passed in the afterbirth.

The sexual organs of the male cat, the testes, lie close to the anus in the tightly attached, furry scrotum. Immediately behind the scrotum is the penis, which points backward. When mating, the male introduces his erect penis into the vagina of the female by strongly curving his body and pushing his pelvis forward.

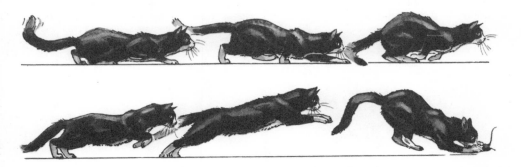

Movement study IV. The sequence of these six drawings shows a cat in pursuit of its prey, starting with the belly-to-the-ground crawl and ending with a deadly pounce.

47

A Cat's Body and What It Can Do

The act of copulation causes ovulation to take place in the female. The ova are released and move through the Fallopian tubes, where they are fertilized, to the uterus.

Sensory Organs

The sensory capacities of cats developed as an adaptation to the animals' original way of life, the life of a hunter. Cats' ears — their acuity is evident in the external appearance of the large, broadly placed, mobile, outer ears — can accurately detect the minutest sounds of prey (peeping of mice, sounds of gnawing) at great distances. They perceive sounds of considerably higher frequencies (up to about 65 kilohertz [kHz]) than those that are audible to humans, whose hearing stops at 20 kHz. It is not surprising that creatures with such a delicate hearing mechanism react with intense displeasure to shrill tones and loud noises that hardly offend the relatively dull human ear.

Once a cat, using its ears for guidance, has gotten close enough to its prey for pouncing, its large, light-sensitive eyes help it make out its target clearly and leap at it with deadly accuracy. In the twilight the pupils open wide, allowing the eyes to make optimal use of whatever light is present. Since their eyes are located at the front of the head, cats have a three-dimensional view and can gauge the position of their prey accurately.

In contrast to their remarkable senses of sight and hearing, the sense of smell is not very well developed in cats.

Cats also have highly sensitive whiskers on the muzzle and above the eyes. These hairs convey sensory stimuli that facilitate spacial orientation.

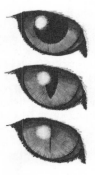

The shape of the pupils also reflects different moods: narrowed pupils signal tension and threat of attack; wide open pupils, fear and readiness to fight.

Cats' eyes react to diminishing light and to darkness by enlarging the pupils (left) and to bright light by narrowing them down to a slit (right).

Professor Paul Leyhausen: Cat Language

Cats' Modes of Expression

Animals come into contact with others in various ways: reproduction and the raising of the young, defining and observing rank, defending territory, and mutual warning against dangers and enemies. All this and much more depends on an animal understanding the moods and intentions of others of its kind, on adapting its own behavior to these cues, and thus influencing the behavior of others in turn. Since animals, unlike humans, have no words to communicate with each other, they use signs of all kinds. This nonverbal communication plays an important role for us humans, too, both as a complement to and a precursor of language.

Most of the signs of "animal language" are transitory: facial expressions, gestures, sounds. Many animals also leave more permanent signs that others of their kind recognize and understand even when their producer is no longer there.

Signs of whatever kind are meaningless if those they are intended for fail to perceive them, observe them, or understand them. Giving and interpreting signals is innate in all animals. At a certain stage of their development, animals can do both without ever having had to learn how. But many birds and mammals expand this innate ability by learning additional repertoires.

All of what I have just said applies to our house cats, too. They have an exceptionally large stock of the most varied forms of expression. You may wonder why such a highly differentiated system of signals evolved in an animal that has the reputation of being an unsociable loner. But mammals, even if they spend most of the year without contact with others of their kind, still have to meet and understand one another during mating, the accompanying encounters with rivals, and the subsequent rearing of young. Also, ethologists, who study animal behavior, have discovered in the past twenty years that cats, including the various wild forms, are by no means as asocial as people used to think. House cats have even advanced way beyond their wild ancestors in their capacity to develop new forms of social organization. This is probably because among domestic animals the cat is a special case. It was not domesticated as the others were, but chose to live with humans of its own free will. But, as far as we can tell, there has been no corresponding increase in the modes of communication within the species. Apparently the original semantic potential of the species has proved adequate for dealing with new forms of coexistence.

Facial Expression

The extremely mobile musculature of nose, lips, cheeks, ears, and forehead, the rapid dilation and narrowing of the pupils, and whiskers that often accentuate the muscle movements around the muzzle — these all combine to create a wide variety of expressions.

Threat of attack. The ears are turned so that their backs are visible from the front; the head is held sideways and slowly sways from side to side at every step; and the eyes are glued on the enemy.

Professor Paul Leyhausen: Cat Language

Ears. Pointed forward, ears convey friendly interest and different degrees of attentiveness or suspense depending on how far up or toward the center they are pulled by the muscles of the forehead (color photographs, page 73, above and lower left). Ears pricked up and turned slightly backward (picture below and color photograph, page 20, lower right) are a warning that attack is imminent. If the ears are also bent back and drawn down sideways, this signals a defensive attitude, fear, and readiness to take flight (color photograph, page 56, upper left).

Cheek ruff. In the mood of excitement and expectation mixed with fear, the cheek muscles pull the cheek ruff downward and toward the throat, sometimes in a pulsing rhythm. This is easy to observe in lynxes and othe types of cat with prominent cheek ruffs. Since in house cats this ruff is hardly longer than the other hair, its movements are not easy to see, and you have to observe the cat very closely to detect them.

Whiskers. The positioning and spreading of the whiskers also contributes to the expressions already mentioned. If the whiskers are pointed forward and fanned out, the cat is tense, attentive, and ready to act; when they point sideways and are less spread out, the cat is calm and comfortable; and when they are bunched together and flattened to the side of the face, the cat is reserved or even shy (picture, next column).

Pupils. Narrowed pupils are a sign of tension, heightened interest, and aggressive threat, whereas dilated pupils express surprise, fear, and a defensive attitude. But since the size of the pupils also depends on the light, the changes due to shifts in mood can be magnified or canceled out by changes in lighting.

Yawning. Yawning is not as contagious in cats as it is in humans. Seeing another cat yawn does not make a cat sleepy. Instead, yawning is more a sign of reassurance, expressing some-

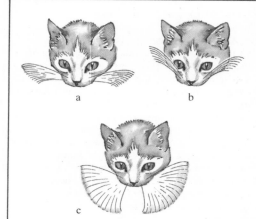

a   b

c

The position of the whiskers shows: (a) relaxation, friendly disposition, satisfaction, or indifference; (b) reserve, timidity, shy curiosity; (c) great excitement, tension, readiness for immediate action.

thing like: "I'm feeling peaceful, and I hope you are too."

Lips. Movements of the lips that serve an expressive purpose are usually combined with sounds and will be discussed in that context. But there are two phenomena that should be mentioned here: *flehmen* (see below) and a strange warning gesture that large felines such as lions and tigers make, but that has not yet been observed in house cats.

Flehmen is a curious grimace cats sometimes display. It was first described and named by the former director of the Leipzig Zoo in Germany, Dr. Karl-Max Schneider. For lack of an original English word, the term flehmen (pronounced "flay-men") has been adopted by the English-speaking world. Flehmen occurs not only in all kinds of felines but in many other mammals as well, for example most hoofed animals.

Professor Paul Leyhausen: Cat Language

Raising the lip. This drawing exaggerates this normally much less obvious expression. Generally the mouth is opened just a little, and the nose barely wrinkled.

The grimace is primarily a response to certain scents of a sexual nature, but other smells can also evoke it. The cat, with its mouth slightly open, draws the corners of its mouth back and the nose and upper lip up. The resulting horizontal and vertical wrinkles give rise to a typical expression that to us looks as if the animal were turning up its nose or expressing displeasure or disgust. In fact it is probably just the opposite. The expression is connected with the functioning of Jacobson's organ, a second organ of smell that is still fully present in cats but has disappeared in many mammals, including primates and humans. In lions and other big cats, the grimace is very pronounced. In house cats, the facial musculature allows for only a faint version of this expression, and it is easily overlooked if one does not consciously watch out for it (see picture).

A second expressive movement of the lips that bears no relation to the production of sound was also described by Dr. Schneider, who termed it a *gesture of embarrassment*. It looks much the same as flehmen, but the mouth either stays closed or is opened only very slightly; the lips are drawn farther back and less far up, and the nose is not wrinkled. At the same time the head swings slowly from side to side. This behavior, which has so far been observed only in the big cats, seems to express friendly rejection of another member of the species that is approaching with equally friendly intentions. Translated into human terms it seems to say something like: "Please be kind and leave me alone for a moment." It is either absent altogether in small cats or is just as unobtrusive as flehmen and has therefore eluded even careful observers. I mention it here for the sake of completeness.

Ears that are raised but twisted to the back, combined with hissing, announce that an attack is in the offing.

Gestures

By gestures we mean positions and movements of head, body, and limbs (including the tails) when they carry a message or serve as a signal. In the case of mammals with fur, the ability to erect the hairs on certain parts of the body or the entire body must also be included.

Head. A head stretched forward indicates readiness for contact; facial expression and other gestures signal whether the encounter is likely to be friendly or antagonistic. A cat that feels dominant raises its head, one that feels inferior lowers it. If the head is lowered more or less jerkily and with the chin pulled in, or if

Professor Paul Leyhausen: Cat Language

When two cats meet, the posture and movements of head, tail, and limbs serve to communicate moods and intentions. The accompanying facial expressions also clarify whether the approach is made in a friendly spirit or not.

the head is turned sideways, the cat is expressing a lack of interest; in an encounter with a strange cat it indicates that the cat wishes neither to provoke nor to be provoked. If the head is raised very high and pulled far back, the cat is trying to avoid encountering another that is being overly persistent.

Legs. Legs stretched to their full length are a sign of self-confidence and even of readiness to attack. Bent hind legs, on the other hand, indicate uncertainty (color photograph, page 128) or even timidity. If the forelegs bend, the cat wants to avoid conflict but would defend itself if necessary. Bent forelegs and hind legs mean uncertainty, caution, and defensiveness.

Body. If the body is stretched, the cat feels sure of itself or prepared to attack. A contracted body or a back arched in typical cat fashion, indicates fear and readiness for defense (picture, right).

Tail. The motions of the tail function as a barometer of the cat's moods. Waving the tail quickly and jerkily from side to side betrays high excitement of various kinds. A still, raised tail is simultaneously a friendly greeting and an invitation to sniff the anal region. If, however, the tail whips up suddenly, this a threat of attack. It is interesting to note that some breeds of cats whose tails are very short, and therefore not very expressive, convey these moods with facial changes instead. The lynx, for instance, moves its cheek ruffs, and the caracal changes the position of its ears and the tufts on them. When the threatening behavior lasts for some time, the tail usually stays still, raised more or less at the base then bent downward like a hook. If the excitement is very great, the tip whips back and forth.

Hair. If the cat is afraid, the hair stands up fairly evenly all over the body. When the cat threatens or is ready to attack, the hair stands up only in a narrow band along the spine and on the tail. In threat and attack the hair not only stands up but also inclines slightly toward the middle from both sides, thus forming a sharp ridge. Forms of hair erection somewhere between the two described also occur.

Vocalization

There are both vocal and nonvocal sound signals.

A young cat play-acting readiness for attack: the slightly arched back and the raised front paw belong to the repertoire of defensive gestures.

Professor Paul Leyhausen: Cat Language

Purring is a nonvocal sound with which everyone is familiar. Purring probably originated as a vocalization of the young to tell the mother that they are content. Producing this sound does not interfere with sucking so that sound contact with the mother can be maintained during nursing. In adult cats, too, purring usually means: "All is well, and I'm feeling fine." But it also acquires other shades of meaning, depending on the situation in which it occurs. A mother cat purrs when she approaches the nest of kittens, assuring them, "It's me, not an enemy." Older kittens purr when they try to get adult cats to play, and dominant ones when they approach inferior ones with peaceful or playful intentions, thus assuaging possible apprehensions. Finally, sick animals hardly able to defend themselves purr in a precautionary effort to soothe a potential aggressor. If one considers this progression of examples attentively, one no longers finds it paradoxical that seriously ill cats, feeling anything but fine, will purr when another cat or a person approaches them.

Hissing. A common nonvocal sound of warning found among many nonaquatic vertebrates is hissing. When cats hiss, they open their mouths about halfway, draw back their upper lips (wrinkling their faces almost as described in flehmen, and arch their tongues high with the rims curving upward picture, page 51). As they do this, they expel their breath so hard that one can feel the air jet if one is close enough. Now you will understand why almost all cats shy away if you blow into their faces. Even the grimace of hissing without audible sound or noticeable air movement succeeds in repulsing. Hissing, then, is a form of expression that affects three different senses: hearing, sight, and touch.

Spitting. Spitting is another warning or threatening sound. This is a sudden and violent nonvocal sound, often accompanied by one or both forepaws hitting the ground. Dangerous and frightening as it may sound, spitting is usually not much more than bluff. The attack it seems to announce usually does not take place, even if the other continues to approach. But in most cases the cat achieves its purpose by spitting. The (supposed) attacker at whom the spitting is aimed shies back for a moment, and the cat has a chance to escape.

Growling. Another kind of sound that is accompanied by a typical facial expression is growling, which—unlike hissing—signals offense rather than defense. The facial difference between these two behaviors is that in growling the corners of the mouth are drawn up more than the upper lip. Repeated spurts of growling turn into *snarling,* which has an impressive effect indeed, particularly when produced by the big cats.

Tooth-Chattering. Tooth-chattering (or lip-smacking) is a nonvocal sound whose precise meaning is not known. Cats utter it when they see prey they want but cannot reach because of some external obstacle. With the mouth opened slightly, the lips are pulled far back and the jaws opened and closed rapidly, producing smacking noises that somewhat resemble the sound of a person's teeth chattering from the cold. If the excitement is very great, the tooth-chattering becomes vocalized, and in time with the jaw movements the cat utters tiny staccato noises faintly reminiscent of the sounds made by a goat's kid.

Properly speaking, this behavior should not be discussed here at all because, though it does express excitement of some kind on the part of the cat that produces it, it does not, as far as we know, evoke any kind of response from other cats. In other words, it seems to have no communicative function.

In addition to these nonvocal sounds, cats

53

also have a repertoire of vocal sounds that can occur in all kinds of variations and therefore take on a variety of meanings.

Meowing. The best known of these sounds is meowing, which probably derives from the call of an abandoned or unhappy kitten. A kitten will emit this call if it somehow got out of the nest and is cold, if the returning mother disturbs it in its sleep, and in other similar situations. In grown cats a short, high meow also signals some kind of discontent, unhappiness, or lack. To a certain extent the same can be said of the mating calls of both sexes, which are a version of meowing.

Gurgling. A high-pitched gurgle is a friendly greeting. If this is combined with gentle meows, it becomes "chatting," a sound that varies in exact quality from cat to cat and is a kind of social contact sound. Some cats will do that for half an hour or more at a time and modulate the sound so much that they hardly ever repeat themselves. This capacity for variation must play an important role in their vocal exchanges, but it has not yet been studied in sufficient depth.

A modified version of gurgling is found in another context. This is the curious call a mother cat makes when she brings the first prey to her four- to five-week-old kittens, urging them to come and have a closer look. If the prey is small and harmless, this call still resembles the gurgling it is based on, but if the prey is large and possibly dangerous, the mother announces this with loud calls that almost resemble screams. For a long time we therefore used to speak of "calling mouse" and "calling rat." But one day, when a door was closed, shutting the mother cat off from her nest and kittens as she was bringing a mouse, the mouse call developed smoothly into rat call.

"Calling mouse" and "calling rat" are, then, really just the two extremes of one and the same vocalization. But ordinarily a cat will not use forms falling between these extremes. Instead she uses the two calls almost like concepts or words for specific things. She calls "mouse" only if she actually has a mouse, and calls "rat" only if she is bringing a rat, or even a piece of rat that may be much smaller than a fat mouse. So the nature of the call is determined by the kind of prey, not by its size.

I described this in such detail because to my knowledge this is the first and only case in which such use of sounds has been observed in a mammal. It implies that the cat can distinguish conceptually between a rat and a mouse without having been taught by humans. The kittens, for their part, clearly respond differently to the two calls. If they hear their mother call "mouse," they come running without fear. A rat, on the other hand, can be a dangerous enemy for small kittens, and when the mother cat calls "rat" the kittens approach the prey reluctantly and cautiously, if at all, at least the first few times.

I am far from saying, of course, that cats are on the verge of developing a language based on words. But I am convinced that up to now the capacity of the more highly developed mammals to convey meaning through vocalization has been underestimated. Examples such as the one I have described easily escape notice. Without the closed door and later analysis of tape recordings, we would no doubt have missed this one too.

A house cat in pursuit of a mouse.   ▷
Above: From his perch, a beam where he had lain in wait, this tomcat is pouncing on his prey with one leap.
Below: Now he gets a sure grip on the mouse with his teeth to carry it somewhere where he can enjoy his meal undisturbed.

Professor Paul Leyhausen: Cat Language

Screeching. When cats are in great distress they utter a screeching cry that some ethologists have called "defensive screeching." This cry is also often emitted at the conclusion of mating. It, too, no doubt evolved from meowing as a strong accentuation of the second syllable.

Caterwauling. Finally there is the well-known caterwauling of tomcats. Usually poetically misinterpreted as a love song, it is in fact a song of threat and war. Rival tomcats emit these sounds as they approach each other in slow motion and on stiff legs during their threat display.

This brief enumeration of the main sounds that house cats are capable of may not at first glance seem to amount to much, but when one discovers the enormous multiplicity of variations there are, one realizes just how wide their vocal repertoire is. This fact gives rise to a number of as yet unanswered questions. We can say generally that mammals, unlike many songbirds, have a complete stock of vocalizations that is innate. House cats, at any rate, can develop these even without the help of feedback via their sense of hearing, which is so essential, for example, to human babies in producing sounds and learning to speak. Even a kitten that is born deaf develops its species' entire normal repertoire of sounds. The fact that numerous individual variations exist nevertheless, seems to suggest that these differences convey different meanings. It is at this point an open question whether or not these differences could be the basis of a system of communication, a kind of group dialect, linking the

members of small groups or neighborhoods. Experiments that could provide clear answers in this area would take a long time and be expensive, so we will probably have to wait for some time before we can attain any certainty on this point.

Scent Signals

Scent signals can take direct effect when two cats meet. When the animals touch, scents may be conveyed directly from one to the other. But cats also deposit scents, primarily through glands in the cheeks and near the anus, on objects where they can still be detected by other cats for several days or even weeks.

Cats, like all mammals, have a *body odor* which, particularly in females, changes with the fluctuations of hormonal production accompanying the reproductive cycle.

There are also more localized *skin glands* in the cheeks and under the chin, on the pads of the feet, and on the lower back near the base of the tail that secrete scents.

Males have an *anal sac* near the anus as well.

The exact role of the secretions from these various glands is not yet very clear. We do know that cats recognize each other by the scents emitted from the glands in the cheeks. It also seems likely that cats spread scents to each other in greetings and social intercourse so that a kind of group scent is produced. Certain forms of physical contact, usually assumed to be merely tactile, play a role here: rubbing against each other with the head, the flanks, and the cheeks (pictures, pages 7 and 60) and running the length of the body under the chin of a partner (picture, page 58). Possibly touching a partner's back with the tail has a similar function (picture, page 61).

All the movements cats perform to touch each other are also executed with suitable objects, and thus the scents are spread to these objects. It has been shown that other cats detect

◁ Cat relatives.
Above left: European wildcat; hissing and flattened ears signal moderate readiness to attack or flee. Above right: African wildcat with kitten. Middle left: Lynx. Middle right: Indian tiger. Below left: African lion. Below right: Cheetahs.

Professor Paul Leyhausen: Cat Language

these scents several days later and still can even recognize which cat left them.

Tomcats in particular have two more ways to spread their scent. As a rule they bury feces and urine as female cats do, but along the border of their territory they often do not. Instead they leave their droppings in spots that somehow stand out, as on bare ground, paths, tree stumps, or rocks.

Another habit of tomcats is well known: this is *spraying,* in which urine is squirted backwards in a jet. Female cats, particularly older ones, may do this, too, but they do it less often. Also, they cannot mix secretions from the anal sac with the urine, which creates that typical tomcat smell that humans find so unpleasant.

When spraying, cats usually stretch their hind legs tall, with the tail pointing straight up and trembling convulsively. They direct their rear end toward a wall, a protruding corner, a post, rock, or bush, and spray diagonally upward at it (picture, page 59).

This young cat is running its back under the chin of an adult cat. Usually the animal thus approached does not raise its chin, as shown here, but presses down more or less firmly on the back that moves along in front of it.

Depending on the weather, the smell may linger for two weeks or more, changing gradually from exposure to oxygen, and finally disappearing. This means that other cats can tell for days just who it was that sprayed and how long ago. Indoors, the smell lasts almost forever, which is why it is practically impossible to keep an unneutered male cat exclusively in an apartment. The uric acid of cats is also very corrosive, affecting iron and many other metals, and it rots wood in the long run and shrivels up the leaves of bushes that are sprayed often.

You can sometimes see male cats rubbing their cheeks against objects they have often sprayed and equipping themselves with a plume of smell that they carry around as the medieval knights carred their colors. Presumably they do this to impress their rivals.

The act of spraying is itself very conspicuous. It functions as an optical signal, but it also affects the animal doing it. After a cat fight, the winner will often spray urine several times in succession in such a way that the vanquished rival is bound to see it. The loser also sprays after a while, but he is careful not to do it in his rival's field of vision. I have always had the impression that in spraying, the inferior animal restores its injured ego, shakes off the feelings of defeat (sometimes it really does shake itself in the intervals between spraying), and regains its equanimity. A cat that sprays in front of an opponent is demonstrating his self-confidence and strength.

Some species of cat also leave another kind of visible mark. They crouch as urinating and scrape the ground with peculiar sweeping motions of the hind paws, sprinkling a few drops of urine into the resulting shallow groove as they do so. The scrape marks are usually located along paths that are much frequented by cats and so stand out from the surrounding area. These visible signs serve to attract the attention of other cats using the paths and cause them to sniff the scent mark deposited there. It is the

Professor Paul Leyhausen: Cat Language

A tomcat spraying. The rear is raised high on straight hindlegs facing a wall, some protrusion, a post, or a bush. The tail points straight up and trembles convulsively.

scent mark that contains the message. However, this behavior has not yet been observed in house cats or their nearest wild relatives. But house cats, like all other species of cat, do sharpen their claws on tree trunks that are lying down or preferably standing up straight or at an angle (picture below). Since they use the same trees over and over again, the bark soon becomes tattered and the scratching spot very obvious. The primary function of sharpening the claws is actually to remove old, worn layers of claw. But cats will often sharpen their claws with special vigor in front of another cat, clearly a demonstration of self-confidence. In the scratch marks the cat leaves behind, it conveys the same message *in absentia*. Whether or not secretions from the sweat glands between the toes also remain and act as signals is still open to debate. It has, however, been observed that cats often sniff such scratching trees intensely.

Expression and Impression

This brief summary of the prime modes of expression of cats hardly conveys the possible range and variety of expressions and the messages they convey. Cats not only display the various elements of expression described above in many gradations of intensity and duration but they also combine them in different ways so that an incredible variety of expressions and combinations of these is created. This wealth of manifestations is not wasted but finds its complement in the equally differentiated capacity of cats to receive and adequately react to impressions. As I have already suggested several times, many expressive signals, viewed in isolation, are ambiguous and acquire a particular meaning in a particular case only from combination with others and from the situation in which the transmitter of the expression and the receiver of the impression are at the time.

Cats do not need to learn the basic repertoire of expressions, and they react adequately to the expressions of other cats without having had previous experience. Much of this repertoire they share with many mammals and even with other vertebrates. Hissing, for instance, is a

Sharpening the claws. When sharpening claws to show off, cats prefer posts or tree trunks that stick up, permitting them to reach up as high as possible.

Professor Paul Leyhausen: Cat Language

warning and defensive sound in many reptiles (lizards, snakes, turtles), birds, and mammals, and all of them understand this sound, even when it is produced by a creature not of their own species. Simulating an increased body size, as by erecting fins, combs, feathers, or fur, is another signal to others that has a frightening effect on vertebrates ranging from fish to humans. I could list many other examples. For this reason, I have referred to an "esperanto of expression" in vertebrates. However, there are also forms of expression that are peculiar to individual species and that can therefore give rise to misunderstandings between members of different species. Any attentive fancier of cats will have noticed that at some times the understanding between felines and humans is totally natural and effortless and yet at others apparently inexplicable misunderstandings arise.

I said above that cats do not have to learn to express themselves and understand others, but

Cats choose any solid objects such as protrusions in walls or posts to rub their cheeks, necks, or sides against.

that does not mean that kittens cannot add to their native abilities. A kitten will soon see, for instance, that the demonstrations of an excitable aunt carry no more weight than the calmer behavior of its more phlegmatic mother, and it learns to use expressions for a purpose. In the process, expressive behavior becomes independent of the mood that gave rise to it originally; the behavior becomes separate and can develop into a kind of deceptive maneuver such as "begging." The deception works because the receptive mechanisms cannot be disconnected as the expressive ones can. The mechanism of impression reacts to the "acted" expression just as automatically as it does to the "real thing." And cats know how to point their expressive behavior in just the right direction. They can, for instance, produce the required facial mime on only one half of their faces, the half that is turned toward the creature they want to convey the message to.

Of course cats, like other animals, also learn to understand the expressions of creatures other than cats for which they have no specific mechanisms of impression. In expression and impression, as in behavior generally, innate and learned elements work smoothly together to produce a unified result.

In this chapter I have as far as possible avoided using a term that has become very popular in recent times, the term "communication." This concept is used and abused in all conceivable contexts. There is hardly anything in the relationship between different members of a species and even of completely unrelated organisms that is not called communication. But a concept that is used so indiscriminately loses practically all its value because it expresses everything and therefore nothing. It would be absurd to speak of communication when a cat leaves its droppings on a rock along the boundary of his territory. Strictly speaking, we should not even use the term "message,"

Professor Paul Leyhausen: Cat Language

Human arrogance has long denigrated the capacities of highly developed animals to "communicate" with each other. Oskar Heinroth, the great ornithologist and pioneer of modern ethology, when asked why animals did not develop a language, is said to have answered, "Because they have nothing to say to each other." This answer may have been somewhat rash. Animals have a great deal to say to each other, and they succeed admirably even without a conceptual language. And considering the case of calling "mouse" and "rat," who will still claim that they are totally incapable of forming concepts?

Begging for food. This young cat is trying to get its mother to relinquish the freshly caught rat. The mother crouches down on her front paws to put down the prey, and the younger animal places its tail firmly over the mother's rump in exactly the spot where the scent glands near the base of the tail are located.

because the cat does the same even when there are no neighbors for whom it could be intended. Nevertheless a cat that passes by will find out that something happened ("cat X marked his territory here") and when ("he was here the day before yesterday"). If the cat is new to the area, he will also learn that "this place is already occupied." Putting this situation in the same category as an intentional address—for example, when a cat purrs to invite another one to play—blurs rather than sharpens our understanding.

Cat Diseases and
How to Keep Your Cat Healthy

A Healthy Cat

A cat of healthy constitution, cared for by understanding people and protected against the major adversitites of life, can live twenty years or more. But a venerable old age like this is the exception rather than the rule, and most cats die sooner.

It is important for cat owners to be aware of the hazards to their pets' health. This way they can take the proper precautions and often prevent the worst.

With the exception of a few relatively rare but serious diseases that start imperceptibly, the basic rule is that a cat that is well fed, has a thick, shiny coat, grooms itself, takes an active interest in the world around it, and responds normally to external stimuli is healthy.

Normal Vital Signs

Temperature: 100 to 102.5°F (37.8 to 39.2°C)

Pulse per minute:
    80 to 150 for older animals
    80 to 175 for young animals
    150 to 200 for kittens

Breaths per minute:
    20 for older animals
    20 to 30 for young animals
    30 to 40 for kittens

Feces: moist and soft, dark gray to brown

Urine: clear and yellow, with an unpleasant odor in the case of sexually mature male cats

How to Keep Your Cat Healthy

Keeping an animal in a manner that suits its nature and taking precautions against the major risks to its life are the keys to the normal development of a kitten into a physically and psychologically healthy cat. Take your new kitten to the veterinarian for a check-up, particularly if it is a stray that is not used to being handled by humans. At this first visit you will get to know the veterinarian somewhat and will be able to tell whether or not he likes to deal with cats. Now you will know how and where you can reach help in case of emergency.

If this is the kitten's first visit to a veterinarian, he will discuss with you the animal's development and state of health as well as how to keep it healthy. Usually some treatment against common internal and external parasites (ear mites, roundworms) is required, and vaccinations can be administered right then or about ten days later.

Health Schedule for Young Cats

Age of cat	What you should observe or do:
9–10 days	Eyes open, watch for inflammation or pus
4–5 weeks	First deworming
7 weeks	Second deworming
8 weeks	First vaccination against distemper
10 weeks	First vaccination against upper respiratory infections
11 weeks	Second vaccination against distemper and first one against rabies (combination vaccine)
12 weeks	Second vaccination against upper respiratory infections

The vaccinations can also be given in different combinations or each one singly. Ask your veterinarian.

Cat Diseases and How to Keep Your Cat Healthy

Health Checks

Part of body	Should	Should not
Eyes	Be clear, bright, open.	Tear, be smeary, show discharge; third eyelid should be retracted, not pulled up over part of eye.
Anus	Be clean.	Be smeared with feces.
Breathing	Be quiet and regular.	Be labored or panting.
Coat	Be smooth, shiny, and clean.	Be dull or greasy; fur should not stand up or be infested with parasites.
Skin	Be dry and smooth.	Be fatty or have dandruff or round, red dots.
Lymph nodes	Feel normal.	Feel swollen.
Nose	Be cool and dry.	Be wet or have whitish or yellowish discharge.
Ears	Be absolutely clean.	Show black, smeary patches (sign of mites) or be red (inflammation).
Pulse	Be regular.	Be too fast or too slow.
Teeth	Be white, without plaque.	Be black or have tartar on them.
Gums	Be light pink.	Be too pale or too red; there should be no bad odor from the mouth.

If you spend some time with your cat every day, look it over, play with it and pet it daily, you will quickly be able to tell whether it is well or whether something is ailing it. Changes also become apparent in the course of feeding the cat and cleaning out the litter box. Even a cat that lives outside catches on quickly to regular feeding times and will turn up promptly for meals, giving you a chance to keep track of how it is doing.

Feeding your cat a proper diet (page 34) is no problem with all the prepared cat foods on the market. Make sure your cat always has fresh drinking water available. For the sake of the cat's health, you should clean its food and water dishes as well as its litter box thoroughly and regularly.

Inform yourself about the possibility of your pet's picking up diseases from contact with other cats (for instance, in mating, at cat shows, or by roaming) and be aware of the most important causes of accidents. If you already have several cats, it is advisable to

Cat Diseases and How to Keep Your Cat Healthy

quarantine newcomers or animals that have some infectious disease.

Most important of all, cats, especially those that are kept singly, need a lot of love and attention from "their people"; this is a crucial factor in keeping them content and healthy.

Necessary Vaccinations

The cat's organism, just like a person's, has the ability to produce protective substances (antibodies) against disease-producing agents (antigens). Vaccination makes use of this ability by introducing into the system antigens that have been weakened or already killed so that they no longer cause disease but still trigger the production of antibodies. In this way protection against a number of diseases is achieved. In order for the immunization to be fully effective, kittens have to be at least eight to twelve weeks old, healthy, and free of parasites. (Deworm the animal two weeks before the planned immunization or have the stool analyzed for endoparasites.)

Feline distemper: There is an effective vaccine against feline distemper, and regular vaccinations are an absolute must (Vaccination schedule, following).

Upper respiratory infections: Immunizing your cat against these infections is more difficult because there is more than one disease-producing agent. Vaccination is advisable primarily if other cats with whom your cat has contact suffer from upper respiratory infections. Also, some boarding places require this vaccination before they will board your cat.

Rabies: All cats that run free should be vaccinated against rabies if for no other

reason than the danger this disease represents to humans. Even if your cat never sets foot outside and is therefore in no danger of infection (by being bitten by an infected animal), the cat needs this vaccination if you plan to travel abroad with her or take her to cat shows. There are combination vaccines that offer protection not only against rabies but also against other diseases, such as distemper. Ask your veterinarian.

Vaccination Schedule

	Basic or initial vaccination		Booster shots
	8–12 weeks old	12 weeks and older	
Distemper	2 vaccinations 2–4 weeks apart	1 vaccination	Repeat vaccination every 2 years
Rabies	2 vaccinations 2–4 weeks apart	1 vaccination	Repeat once a year
Upper respiratory infections	2 vaccinations 2–4 weeks apart	2 vaccinations 2–4 weeks apart	Repeat once a year

Basic or First Immunizations

If a kitten is under twelve weeks old, vaccines injected into its body can be neutralized by antibodies still present in its system from the mother, if the mother acquired immunization either through undergoing the disease or through vaccination. This applies to both distemper and rabies, and that is why, if the kitten is under twelve weeks old, a second vaccination is required after two to four weeks for these diseases. In older kittens, one vaccination provides basic protection. Immunization against upper respiratory infections requires

Cat Diseases and How to Keep Your Cat Healthy

Signs of Illness

This is what you notice \ Possible cause	Disorders of the upper respiratory system	Blockage of the intestine	Kidney stones	Distemper	Wrong diet	Infectious peritonitis	Fleas	Foreign bodies	Uterine infection	Hair balls	Leukemia	Nephritis	Fungus	Head cold	Shock	Rabies	Poisoning	Worms	Dental problems
Lack of appetite	•	•	•	•		•	•	•	•	•	•	•	•	•	•	•	•	•	•
Breathing difficulties	•							•			•			•	•		•	•	
Diarrhea			•							•	•				•		•	•	
Increased thirst			•						•		•	•					•		
Vomiting		•	•			•		•	•	•	•				•		•	•	•
Fever	•						•			•		•		•					
Weight loss	•	•	•	•	•	•	•	•	•	•	•	•		•		•	•	•	•
Changes in the skin				•									•						
Coughing	•							•											
Swollen lymph nodes	•										•			•					•
Pallor of mucous membranes			•		•				•		•	•			•		•	•	
Swelling of the body				•			•	•			•								
Abnormal behavior	•	•	•	•	•	•	•	•	•	•	•	•	•	•	•	•	•	•	•
Constipation		•	•			•		•							•		•		

The accompanying table lists some symptoms that may be present in the case of the illnesses indicated. Since symptoms are often atypical, this table is nothing more than a list of possibilities. Use it for watching your pet carefully but do not try to draw conclusions from it. Instead, consult the veterinarian if you suspect illness.

two similarly spaced doses regardless of the kitten's age. Booster shots require only one injection, and the booster for distemper is needed only once every two years. If your veterinarian uses combination vaccines, the cat will get a shot once a year.

Symptoms of Disease

Illness can manifest itself in loss of appetite, sudden loss of weight, changes of behavior, apathy, neglect of grooming (sudden uncleanliness), dull fur, loss of hair, itching, swelling of the body, constant vomiting, increased thirst, or diarrhea. If you observe any of these signs, take the animal to a veterinarian without delay.

Diseases Infectious to Humans

Although there are number of pathogens that affect both cats and humans, the health hazard that domestic cats represent should not be exaggerated. If the animal was dewormed when young and is fed only cooked or commercial food, the danger of contagion is minimal.

Even a cat that spends time outdoors and is therefore more exposed to infections and parasites hardly represents a threat to human health as long as some precautions are taken and basic rules of hygiene are observed.

Theoretically, the following diseases and parasites can be transmitted to humans: ringworm (page 71), rabies (page 79), toxoplasmosis (page 69), roundworm larvae (page 68), and fleas (page 67).

In rare cases it is possible that feline diseases caused by bacteria may present a slight risk of infection to humans. Tuberculosis is a serious disease that can be transmitted from humans to cats and, under certain conditions, vice versa. But thanks to systematic measures taken against it, this disease has been brought under control in most First World countries.

Another problem to be mentioned here is *lymphoreticulosis benigna.* This is not a feline disease at all but a very rare and not yet fully understood virus infection that has been observed in humans and that can apparently be transmitted through scratch wounds, especially cat scratches. The illness is characterized in humans by a swelling of the lymph nodes; no fatalities have been reported.

There is no proof that infectious diseases affecting cats, such as leukemia, can be transmitted to humans. The human organism is basically capable of defending itself against pathogens, and complete isolation is neither necessary nor possible. Generally speaking, the risk a cat represents is insignificant compared to that provided by our normal daily surroundings and, especially, by other human beings.

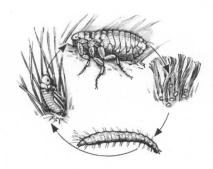

Developmental stages of a cat flea. Starting out as an egg in the cat's fur or as a larva that drops to the ground and feeds on debris and dirt, the creature eventually develops into a full-grown cat flea.

Cat Diseases and How to Keep Your Cat Healthy

Parasites and How to Deal with Them

Ectoparasites

Fleas. Like most other animals, cats sometimes suffer from blood-sucking fleas (more so if they are kept unhygienically). The flea larvae drop to the ground where they feed on dirt and grow in cracks of the floor or in the pet's bed. There are specific cat fleas *(Ctenocephalus felis),* but cats can also be attacked by dog fleas and others, such as bird fleas. Flea powders and flea collar (available from veterinarians) contain substances effective for controlling the blackish fleas, which measure about 1/16 inch (2 mm) and jump off their hosts in big leaps. (Be careful if you put a flea collar on a cat that goes outside; the collar may catch somewhere.) Since the flea eggs are not killed at first exposure to the medication, the treatment has to be repeated at one-week intervals. Some additional hygienic measures are necessary: change the cat's bed frequently, and clean the rooms thoroughly. Insecticides that are safe for cats have also proved effective, but they should not be used near kittens.

Many animals that have had fleas over a period of time develop an allergy to these pests that may cause a *flea eczema* that requires treatment by the veterinarian. Cat fleas do attack humans but are unable to survive long on them or to multiply. They are therefore more of a nuisance than a danger, manifesting themselves by crawling around and by causing unpleasantly itchy bites.

Lice. These yellowish insects, about half as big as fleas, can be detected by the naked eye as they move around in the cat's fur. Although cat lice do not affect humans, they should be combatted in cats. Use the same measures as for fleas.

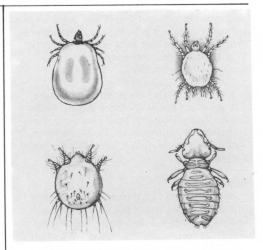

Ectoparasites of cats, some of which are visible only with the help of a magnifying glass. Above left: tick. Above right: ear mite. Below left: mange mite. Below right: biting louse.

Ticks. Cats that go outside may occasionally pick up ticks, which bite into the skin, hold on, and suck blood. Ticks are shiny gray and can be as large as a pea. They are often found on the cat's head, but can also appear on other parts of the body. If you find a tick, dab it with oil and pull it out with tweezers, which should be placed as close to the cat's skin as possible so that the head is removed along with the rest of the tick. If the head tears off, inflammation may follow. You can use special tick pliers instead of tweezers. (Tick oil and pliers are available at pet stores.)

Mites. Finally, the cat is subject to attacks by various kinds of mites, which cause mange. Mites penetrate into the deeper layers of the skin, burrow tunnels, and multiply by laying eggs. In the process they destroy the tissue

67

Cat Diseases and How to Keep Your Cat Healthy

and cause infections. The places begin to itch intensely and later get wet; the skin gets encrusted, and the hair falls out. Any mange attack should be treated repeatedly with appropriate medications.

Ear Mites. These are relatively common. Ear mites are the likely cause if a cat keeps itching and shaking its head (page 76). The formation of scabs can also indicate mites. If you suspect mites, take your cat to the veterinarian.

Endoparasites

Roundworm. This common parasite can be transmitted to a kitten in the mother's milk. Grown cats get infected with roundworms primarily by picking up the eggs off the ground and licking them off their fur. The larvae hatch in the cat's stomach, make their way through the stomach wall, and wander to the liver. From there they are transported by the blood to the lungs, climb up the trachea, are swallowed again and return to the intestinal tract. Now they grow into worms (ascarids) 3

to 4 inches (8. 10 cm) long within three weeks. The sexually mature ascarids lay eggs (up to 200,000 per day), which are eliminated with the feces, survive for months on the ground or in cracks of the floor and are picked up again by the cat. Mice harboring roundworm larvae also act as intermediary hosts (picture below left). The veterinarian can determine if there are worm eggs in the cat's stool. If a cat is heavily infested, it may throw up worms; other signs are a shaggy coat, loss of weight, or a swollen belly. If humans absorb roundworm eggs, the larvae can wander through the organism for a time, but the danger is much smaller than in the case of dog roundworms. In any case, it is important for your cat's health that you have the veterinarian check the animal for worms and prescribe medication if necessary.

Tapeworm and hookworm. In addition to roundworm, cats can get dangerous, bloodsucking hookworms and tapeworms. Cat tapeworms (picture below) grow up to 3 feet (1 m) in length and consist of many small segments, which, thickly covered with eggs, are passed

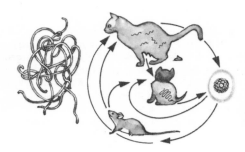

Life cycle of the roundworm. Adult cats generally pick up the eggs of roundworms, but kittens often get the worms through their mother's milk. Laboratory tests of cat feces can determine whether the animal has roundworms or not.

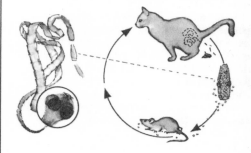

Life cycle of a tapeworm. Cats usually get tapeworms by eating infested mice. The worm segments, which look like grains of rice, are passed in cat feces. Laboratory analysis of a cat's feces also tells whether the animal has tapeworms.

Cat Diseases and How to Keep Your Cat Healthy

with the stool. The most common tapeworm found in cats is absorbed by the cat when it eats infected mice, for mice are the carriers of tapeworm larvae. More rarely, cats get a kind of tapeworm that is transmitted by fleas. The flea larvae eat tapeworm eggs that hatch and are still present in the adult flea. If a cat catches such a flea and chews and swallows it, a new tapeworm grows in its intestines. Sometimes you can spot a segment of a tapeworm that was passed by the cat sticking in the hair near the anus. It looks somewhat like a grain of rice. If you are not sure whether or not it is in fact part of a tapeworm, ask your veterinarian. There are effective and save medications against all kinds of worms that he can prescribe for your cat.

Toxoplasmosis. This disease can run its course unrecognized as an intestinal disorder in which oocysts that are infectious to both animals and humans are excreted over a short period of time (a few weeks) in the stool. The more common way in which the disease is contracted is through the consumption of raw meat that contains toxoplasma oocysts (usually pork in the case of humans and prey in the case of cats). If a cat never gets raw meat to eat and has no contact with the feces of other cats, it is not likely to get toxoplasmosis. This is one more reason for disposing of cat feces promptly and hygienically.

Toxoplasmosis is caused by a one-celled organism *(Toxoplasma gondii)* that reproduces in the tissue cells of higher animals, killing the cells in the process. What is remarkable about this parasite is how unspecific its hosts are. Not only wild animals but also domestic ones and humans can be infected with *Toxoplasma*. In spite of frequent infections, clearly recognizable serious cases of toxoplasmosis are extremely rare.

In humans, toxoplasmosis usually occurs without any external signs. The organism develops antibodies which suppress the disease. But toxoplasmosis does represent a hazard for unborn children whose mothers contract the disease for the first time during pregnancy. This is why pregnant women should use caution in handling cats. To be on the safe side, one can have one's toxoplasmosis antibody titer or level analyzed. This means that a sample of blood serum is thinned until the presence of these antibodies can still, but just barely, be determined. A titer of 1:100 would mean, then, that antibodies still show up in a solution that consists of one part blood serum and 100 parts of diluting liquid. The higher the titer, the more antibodies are in the blood.

Even if the human body has a sufficiently high antibody titer, *Toxoplasma* organisms still remain present in the tissues as so-called oocysts, but they are no longer able to reproduce and are therefore harmless. Almost all people who handle animals a lot or like rare meat have an adequate *Toxoplasma* antibody titer.

Accidents and Injuries

Cats, especially cats that roam outside, run many risks of injury. The traffic on our roads represents the greatest danger. Injuries caused by cars are often so grave that the cat dies instantly. But sometimes a fatally wounded cat somehow manages to drag itself home before it dies. If the owner finds his pet dead near his front door without signs of external injuries he often assumes that it has been poisoned. But a cat that was hit or run over by a car often sustains injuries to internal organs or large blood vessels, injuries that are not externally apparent. Even if help is prompt, the animal usually cannot be saved. If the injuries

Cat Diseases and How to Keep Your Cat Healthy

are external, such as cuts, bruises, or broken bones, the cat has a good chance of recovery. It is even justifiable to keep a loved pet alive by amputating a crushed or partially severed leg. These animals adjust quickly to their handicap and move safely and well on three legs.

There are people with air rifles or small caliber rifles who shoot at cats out of thoughtlessness or because they disapprove of the cat's roaming and its supposed poaching activities.

Uncastrated male cats that roam free and often stray far from home are in greatest danger. Injuries sustained in battles with rivals are usually not too severe, but fights with dogs can have more serious results.

Cats that are kept indoors all the time are less likely to get injured. But it still happens quite often that a cat that is trying to get outside or back in gets caught and squashed in a casement window. If it is not released quickly it may suffocate or die of a spinal injury.

Falling from a great height, as from a window sill or a balcony, is another danger. Although cats have the ability to right themselves in the air so that they land on their feet (figure right) and absorb the shock of the impact, falls still may result in serious injury when, for instance, a physically not very fit apartment cat hurtles down from a third-story window to a concrete floor.

Minor external injuries, such as scratches, small cuts, and bruises, usually heal well and quickly without any special treatment. Cuts, bites, or larger tears in the skin require the veterinarian's attention to heal properly. Foreign bodies in eyes, nose, and ears, and shot from air rifles that has penetrated the skin should also be removed by the veterinarian.

A cat that has undergone a serious accident is often in a state of shock and should be kept undisturbed in a quiet place until the veterinarian arrives. He will then decide what if any emergency measures should be taken.

Movement study V. This sequence of seven drawings shows how a cat, falling with its back to the ground, rights itself by turning 180° before landing on all four feet.

Cat Diseases and How to Keep Your Cat Healthy

Poisoning

Cats get poisoned quite rarely, but some fatal infectious diseases can result in death so quickly that the owner may think his cat has been poisoned. For cats that wander in gardens there is a chance that they might absorb some poison used for rodent control. But with the anticoagulent substances generally used today, a cat would have to eat quite a few poisoned mice to get sick. Cats have a marked distaste for spoiled food, and the gastric acid in their stomachs is highly effective in counteracting the bacteria that cause food poisoning. Hence, chances of getting poisoned this way are extremely slim.

The poisonous substance a cat is most likely to come in contact with in its life with humans is phenol, an ingredient in disinfectants. Pesticides, antifreeze, and certain plants also contain poisons, and contact with heating oil can have serious and even fatal consequences. If you notice that your cat is covered with oil, clean it immediately and thoroughly—first with warmed paper towels, then with a warm bath—so that the oil has no chance to penetrate to the skin or be licked off the fur. Then see the veterinarian.

Disorders of the Skin

Cats suffer from disorders of the skin much less often than dogs. Apart from flea eczema (page 67), there are a few allergic reactions cats are subject to, and they are usually caused by food or factors in the environment that are often overlooked. Bacterial diseases are rare and usually appear as secondary reactions to some other disorder of the skin. Skin problems can also be the result of hormonal imbalances or internal disorders. In any case, the veterinarian should be consulted in cases of prolonged abnormality of the skin.

Ringworm. Ringworm is caused by a fungus of the skin and can be transmitted to humans. Symptoms in cats are hair loss and some usually not very severe itching, but ringworm can be present without these signs, too. If there is any suspicion of ringworm, the veterinarian should be consulted. Getting rid of ringworm is a complicated business; internal as well as external treatments, together with disinfecting measures have to be continued over a period of time.

Acne. Acne, which is a chronic inflammation of the sebaceous glands, occasionally occurs in cats, usually affecting only the lips and chin. It is probably caused by uncleanliness in eating. If it persists, brownish black scabs will form on the reddened skin. Cleaning the affected area carefully every day is an important adjunct to the treatment prescribed by the veterinarian.

Disorders of the Mouth and Teeth

Older cats in particular often form *tartar* on their teeth. This condition can get so serious that a grayish white to brownish layer covers all the teeth, causing bad mouth odor and chronic inflammation of the gums (gingivitis).

In bad cases of tartar or *calculus,* the cat has to be anesthetized for the calculus to be removed with an ultrasound device. Feeding your cat a varied diet, including dry food or fresh bone matter, has some prophylactic effect. But in some cat families, a tendency to develop calculus seems to be inherited, and even young cats are affected by the disorder.

Gingivitis or inflammation of the gums, can be recognized by the bluish red color and by frequent bleeding of the gums and occasionally by pussy sores. Treatment is complicated

Cat Diseases and How to Keep Your Cat Healthy

and involves not only medical therapy but also the removal of the calculus and often of the affected teeth. In severe cases, the condition can be cured only by pulling all the teeth.

Serious illnesses of the liver and kidneys sometimes contribute to chronic gingivitis and to bad odor from the mouth.

Diseases of the Gastrointestinal Tract

Diseases affecting the stomach and intestines or the liver and pancreas usually manifest themselves in one or several of the following symptoms: diarrhea, constipation, vomiting, and lack of appetite.

None of these symptoms gives any clue as to the seriousness of the disorder. Sometimes they are superficial and disappear again with little or no treatment. But at other times they indicate the onset of a serious, perhaps life-threatening or incurable illness.

Diarrhea. Any upset of the digestive system can give rise to diarrhea, especially in young cats. But as long as the general behavior of the animal is not affected, there is no reason to worry. Removing all food for a day or two and letting the cat drink as much clean water as it likes usually clears up the problem. But before resuming normal feeding — omitting raw liver and milk — you should offer the cat only small amounts of cooked meat, cooked liver, or dry or canned cat food. If the diarrhea returns, consult the veterinarian.

It is a serious mistake to try to combat diarrhea by withholding water. Diarrhea and vomiting cause the organism to lose a lot of fluid, and this loss has to be made up for by drinking, or the cat may die quickly. Diarrhea can also indicate the presence of parasites or of some serious illness like distemper. If it persists and is accompanied by listlessness and a

dulling of the fur, it is high time to take action. Diarrhea that lasts for days inevitably leads to dehydration, a condition you can recognize by taking a fold of the cat's skin between your fingers. If it does not smooth out immediately when let go, the cat is severely dehydrated. A potentially fatal loss of body fluid and of the salts suspended in it (electrolytes) has to be counteracted by intravenous injection of fluids.

Constipation. Irregularities in the digestive process can also manifest themselves in constipation. The cat keeps going to her box, trying repeatedly, sometimes for days, to empty her bowels by straining with all her might. If she does not succeed for a considerable length of time, the belly gets noticeably enlarged and the cat loses her appetite. Older long-haired cats are particularly prone to this disorder, and lack of exercise seems to contribute to it. In many cases constipation can be relieved by giving the cat fresh milk, raw liver, or raw spleen. Gently massaging the abdomen and giving an enema (Fleet®, never just water) also help sometimes. If none of these home remedies work, call the veterinarian.

Vomiting. Newcomers to the world of cats worry sometimes when they see their pets throw up. Actually, cats vomit quite easily and painlessly, and many cats deliberately eat grass and other plants to induce vomiting. There is no reason for concern if your cat throws up occasionally after too rich a meal or after eating some grass. People also some-

Common types of house cats.
Above: Black and white male.—the position of the ears indicates that the cat is moderately interested.
Below left: House cat with tiger markings—the ears signal alertness and tension.
Below right: Tricolored house cat.

Cat Diseases and How to Keep Your Cat Healthy

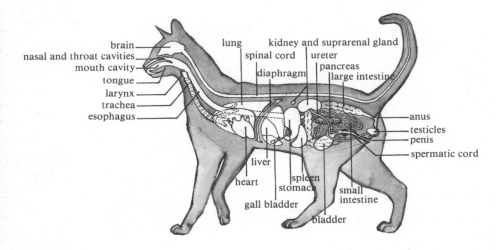

The internal organs of a cat. Digestive tract and teeth are adapted for meat eating. Heart and lungs are in the pectoral cavity, which is separated from the abdominal cavity by the diaphragm.

times mistake the noises and retching that precede vomiting for coughing. If the animal vomits after every meal; however, this is a sign of illness, and the animal has to be examined by a veterinarian.

External Disorders of the Eyes and Nose

Cats frequently suffer from inflammations of the conjunctiva and of the mucous membranes of the nasal cavity. These disorders belong under the general heading of colds and are usually caused by various microorganisms of the *Chlamydia* and *Mycoplasma* genera,

some of which apparently multiply with great rapidity in warm summer weather. In young cats particularly, inflamed conjunctiva often develop pus caused by secondary bacterial infectious agents (bacteria that attack tissues already affected by the previously mentioned microorganisms). The eyelids and areas around the eyes then swell up, and the eyelids and lashes get so sticky with discharge that sometimes the animal can no longer open its eyes. On farms whole litters of kittens with these symptoms finally die of debilitation. Conjunctivitis of this type usually does not respond to merely topical treatment with salves and eye drops; it requires extended general treatment by the veterinarian as well as good general care of the sick animal and a nutritious diet.

◁ Nils and his two house cats Murkel and Mio.

Cat Diseases and How to Keep Your Cat Healthy

Respiratory Infections

Nasal discharge and noisy breathing caused by an accumulation of phlegm in the air passages are often the first sign of a respiratory infection. If the trachea and the larynx are affected as well, there is often coughing and shortness of breath, too. Whenever there is an infection of the air passages, there is a danger that pneumonia may follow. Pneumonia is usually accompanied by high fever and general apathy, and can lead to the death of the animal.

Diseases of the Ears

The most common disorder of the ears in cats is *Otitis externa,* the inflammation of the external ear canal. It is usually caused by mites, measuring 0.3 to 0.5 mm and belonging to the genus *Otodectes.* One sometimes gets the impression that in some areas almost all the kittens and adult cats that go outside suffer from ear mites. In some cases a cat can be a carrier of ear mites for a long time without giving any outward sign of this, while in other, weaker animals with less resistance, an attack of ear mites quickly develops into a serious condition.

From the very beginning of the infestation, the cat is plagued with intense itching and keeps scratching and shaking its head. The light-colored, mobile mites can be detected with an otoscope. Increased exudation of cloudy lymph fluid and large amounts of ear wax mixed with excretions from the mites form brownish black, smeary patches and, later, thick crusts inside the ears. This is an ideal environment for bacteria, and more rarely for fungi, to grow in, and sometimes the infection is perpetuated by these secondary pathogens after the ear mites have died off.

Dirty ears should never be ignored but should be considered a sign of some abnormal condition. If an infection of the external ear canal is attended to promptly, it usually can be cured with the appropriate ear drops. Cleaning out the ear canal with a cotton swab also helps the healing process.

Clean the ears of a cat with a cotton swab dipped into warm water but do not insert it too deeply into the ear canal. This procedure is best undertaken by two people because the cat has to be held securely and still.

The presence of a foreign object (chaff, for instance) in the ear canal can also cause inflammation. In such cases, the object has to be removed by a veterinarian.

If the inflammation spreads to the middle or inner ear, the cat holds its head at a tilt and has trouble keeping its balance.

Cats are subject not only to the gradual deafness that accompanies old age but also to an innate deafness that is genetically passed on. White cats with blue eyes are particularly subject to this latter kind of deafness.

Cat Diseases and How to Keep Your Cat Healthy

Diseases of the Kidneys and the Urinary Tract

Male cats, both castrated and noncastrated, often develop urolithiasis (formation of small "stones" in the urinary tract). The reasons for this are not yet entirely understood. Improper diet plays an important role here, but bacterial or viral agents are also suspected. In male cats, the passing of these stones from the bladder to the urethra often leads to partial or complete blockage of the urinary canal and thus causes a painful accumulation of urine. The affected animal keeps trying, often despite obvious pain, to pass urine. In an attempt to alleviate the discomfort, the cat keeps licking the tip of the penis until it sometimes gets to be a bluish red. Occasionally there is also blood in the urine. If the urinary canal is closed off completely, the animal dies of uremia (an accumulation of poisonous substances in the blood). If any cat, male or female, suffers from urolithiasis, treatment by the veterinarian is necessary. Uremia often occurs as well in older cats suffering from chronic kidney disease. If such a condition is detected early enough, special diets can sometimes prolong the cat's life. (There is a canned cat food designed for cats likely to develop stones that you can obtain through your veterinarian.)

Infection of the Uterus

Sometimes female cats suffer from uterine infection, or pyometra. Pus and sometimes runny matter collects in the uterine horns, a condition that is sometimes, but not always, made manifest by a vaginal discharge. Pyometra is not necessarily caused by a pathogen; it can also be the result of hormone imbalances. It occurs with greater frequency in cats that have had hormone treatment or that were in heat over an extended period of time without having mated or conceived.

Signs of this disease are increased thirst, swelling of the abdomen, lack of appetite, and in many cases a discharge from the vulva that the cat licks off frequently. At a more advanced stage, the cat becomes apathetic, and the fur gets dull. If there is no intention to breed the cat, the best cure is an operation in which the diseased uterus and the ovaries are removed.

Neutering female cats while they are healthy is the best way to prevent diseases of the uterus.

Diseases of the Blood and Cardiovascular System

Unlike dogs, cats rarely suffer from cardiovascular insufficiencies (a heart too weak to supply the organism with sufficient blood and oxygen). And because of the cat's sedentary way of life, this kind of heart failure is usually not detected in cats. However, if sudden exertion is required, a grave state can develop quickly. A bluish discoloration of the mucous membranes and accumulations of fluid in the lungs or the peritoneum (ascites) are symptoms of serious heart disease.

Anemia is common in cats and can have a number of causes. Leukemia (page 79) is often accompanied by anemia, and there are bacterium-like parasites in the blood cells that cause anemia. Anemia can also result from some serious internal disease or from blood poisoning (sepsis).

Noticeable pallor of the mucous membranes (as of the conjunctiva or the gums), fast pulse and breathing (above 40 breaths per minute and a pulse higher than 150), and general apathy are always cause for alarm, and you

Cat Diseases and How to Keep Your Cat Healthy

should take your cat to be examined by a veterinarian when you see any of these signs. Of course, if the diagnosis is leukemia, no treatment offers any hope.

Infections

Cats are affected by many common disease-causing bacteria, but there are hardly any bacterial diseases that are specific to cats. Cats generally catch diseases when they eat infected prey or come in contact with sick animals or their excreta. Quite often, too, infections are secondary to external injuries (accidents, bites).

Blood Poisoning (Sepsis). In a localized inflammation there is always the danger that the infecting agent may penetrate into the blood stream and cause blood poisoning. The first sign of such poisoning is high fever. Apathy follows, and death may result quickly if effective treatment is not initiated immediately.

Tuberculosis. With the increased health standards for cattle, general improvement of hygiene and diet, and the reduction of tuberculosis in humans, tuberculosis in cats has become rare. Still, it occurs now and then, and when it does it also represents a danger to humans. For this reason, any cat that has contracted tuberculosis should be put to sleep.

Viral Infections

Serious viral infections are the most common cause of death in cats. Resistant as these animals are to external injuries and falls, they are very susceptible to viral diseases.

Feline Distemper (Panleukopenia). This is the most common viral disease afflicting cats

and probably claims more victims than any other disease. The first vaccines developed for cats were those for distemper. The period between first contact with the disease and its outbreak is about one week.

Symptoms of a typical case are: diarrhea, vomiting, pains in the abdomen (the animal complains when its belly is touched), apathy, fever, and loss of fluid leading to dehydration. Death follows quickly. An analysis of the blood reveals a rapid decrease in the number of white corpuscles. This fact is responsible for the scientific name for the disease, panleukopenia, decrease of white blood cells or leucocytes.

To have any chance of recovery, cats with distemper must be given transfusions of serum and electrolytes immediately. The distemper virus is very resistant and can still cause disease after years of dormancy. Thorough disinfection with formaldehyde (a 5 percent solution of formalin) is therefore important, but is next to impossible in any normal apartment. The preventive immunization of all cats is therefore highly recommended, but female cats should not be vaccinated while they are pregnant because the vaccine can cause brain damage in unborn kittens.

Although the viruses causing canine and feline distemper are very similar (vaccines for feline distemper have been shown to be effective in dogs), there is no danger of the disease being passed on from one kind of animal to the other.

Upper Respiratory Infections. This heading covers a number of different infections of the sinuses, nose, and bronchia that can be caused by various viruses. The manifestations range from fairly harmless eye colds with occasional sneezing to very serious illnesses that can result in death.

Affected animals need intensive care, preferably in their familiar surroundings, and, in severe cases, an extended therapy of antibiotics and frequent infusions of fluids. There are vaccines against the most dangerous viruses (for example, the herpes virus). Viruses causing respiratory infections in cats die quickly in the open air, but they persist in the recuperating cat so that an apparently healthy cat can still pass the infection on to others.

Leukemia. Feline leukemia is also caused by a virus. This virus can be transmitted, particularly to kittens, by cats with no obvious symptoms of the disease. Leukemia can take many different forms. In the most serious cases there are swellings of the lymph nodes, and anemia (page 77) that ultimately leads to death. Over 80 percent of the tumors found in cats are caused by lymphocytic leukemia. Because leukemia also affects and weakens the body's immune system, cats afflicted with it are very susceptible to other pathogens as well. In leucocytic leukemia the disease affects only the blood and manifests itself externally in anemia. Because the disease is so contagious, all cats that have been diagnosed as having leukemia should be kept in complete isolation from other cats. There is no indication that feline leukemia can be transmitted to humans. There are laboratory tests available that detect the presence of leukemia, and it is advisable to have your veterinarian check your cat for the disease.

Infectious Peritonitis. This is usually a chronic disorder accompanied by progressive ascitis. But infectious peritonitis can also take an atypical course without external symptoms and lead quickly to death.

Signs that may indicate the disease are: emaciation, accumulation of fluid in the abdominal and pectoral cavities, lack of appetite, lethargy, fever, and tumorous changes in various body tissues.

No effective therapy has been discovered yet, and the disease is therefore incurable. It is also not clear yet under what conditions the disease is transmitted and why some cats succumb to it while others do not.

Rabies. Cases of rabies have to be reported. Rabies is a viral disease that at this point primarily affects foxes. It is transmitted if a rabid animal bites another warm-blooded animal or a human being. The incubation period (the time between the infection and the occurrence of symptoms) can be several months. Once the disease breaks out with its symptoms of changed behavior or paralysis, it is impossible to cure and always ends in death.

Because of its danger to humans, the disease has acquired a lot of notoriety, but it occurs quite infrequently in cats. Still, all cats that go outdoors should have rabies shots once a year.

Aujeszky's Disease. Periodically, this virus disease, which primarily attacks pigs and must be reported, receives attention when dogs and cats are killed by it. The course of Aujeszky's disease often resembles that of rabies. Often, but not always, the affected animal suffers from itching. The disease, like rabies, always ends in death and can attack many different animals, but human beings are apparently immune to it. As a precautionary measure against infection, cats should be fed no raw or undercooked pork or raw butcher's scraps.

If an animal dies of an unrecognized illness, an autopsy should be performed by a veterinary laboratory. This is especially advisable if the animal was kept with others.

Cat Diseases and How to Keep Your Cat Healthy

A Visit to the Veterinarian

Any well-cared-for cat will have to make several trips to the veterinarian's office in the course of its lifetime, if only to get the necessary immunizations and occasional health checks, and, in many cases, to be neutered. If possible, find a veterinarian who is not too far away and seems to like dealing with cats. The treatment of cats rarely requires specialized equipment such as x-ray machines, and the presence or absence of such equipment should not determine your choice of a veterinarian. In case your cat should need specialized medical equipment, it may be sent to an animal clinic. I would also advise you not to change veterinarians unless necessary: a veterinarian who knows your cat and its history is in a better position to treat it, and a good relationship between the veterinarian and the owner can develop.

When you take your cat to the veterinarian, transport it in an escape-proof carrier; a sturdy box of heavy cardboard with a top will do if necessary (do not forget to cut air holes). The cat will feel relatively safe and secure in the carrier, particularly if familiar with it from home. Shopping bags or open cardboard boxes or baskets will not do for carrying a cat. Nor should you carry your cat in your arms from the car to the office unless the cat is secured by a leash. Many a cat has escaped between car and office door and made a panicked dash for freedom.

If your cat is sick, your veterinarian will be grateful if you can describe as accurately and objectively as possible the symptoms you have observed. It is also a good idea to take the cat's temperature (you can find out how to do it on page 81) before you set out to see the veterinarian.

Looking after a Sick or Recuperating Cat

A cat suffering from a severe illness or recuperating from an operation that has left it weak and listless needs intensive and understanding care. The cat should have a clean bed (cardboard carton with low sides or a flat basket) in a familiar and quiet place. It is easier to treat the patient if this "sickbed" is on a table or some other raised place.

More important than food for a sick cat is the regular intake of fluids, and you therefore must make sure that the cat drinks enough. Many illnesses and especially diarrhea and vomiting (page 72) lead to a progressive loss of fluid and dehydration that has to be combatted by the veterinarian through the injection of electrolyte solutions.

If the cat is unable to eat food on its own for some time, it has to be fed. If the cat refuses to swallow even favorite foods, you should try feeding it some homemade bouillon (without seasonings) with a syringe (turn to page 81 to find out how to do it) or beef serum if the veterinarian recommends it. If the cat is so sick that it cannot keep itself clean, you will have to wipe it after it eats and passes stool. You can also brush the cat carefully if touching causes no pain. But what is more important than anything else for a sick cat is that it be shown affection without any display of nervousness. Cats generally make poor patients, and often even those most familiar with them succeed in measuring their temperature or in getting them to accept medication only with great expense of time and patience and sometimes only by using some force.

Giving Medicines

To give a cat pills or capsules, lift its head up slightly and pry the mouth open. Push the medication in as far as possible, then clamp

Cat Diseases and How to Keep Your Cat Healthy

the mouth shut and hold it that way while you stroke the cat's throat with the other hand to make it swallow. As long as the cat will still eat, stick the pill in a little piece of meat. If the pill is large, cut it up, and put the pieces in a number of meat clumps.

Liquid medications (as well as the bouillon mentioned above) are best administered with a plastic syringe. Hold the head up slightly as described above and squirt the contents of the syringe into the space between the cheek and the back molars. Sometimes cats that refuse to swallow medications forced on them will lick the medicine off their paws quite happily.

Taking a cat's temperature is best done with an assistant. If the cat resists, its front and hind legs have to be held firmly.

Taking the Temperature

The easiest way to take a cat's temperature is to have someone there to help you by holding the cat's shoulders and front legs while you deal with the thermometer. But you can also do it by yourself as shown in the picture above. Lift the cat's tail up somewhat and introduce the lightly lubricated thermometer into the anus. Leave it in for about two minutes. Talk to the cat soothingly and pet it during the ordeal.

A Medicine Cabinet for Cats

Having a special medicine cabinet for cats is important primarily for those who keep a number of animals or have a cat with specific recurrent health problems. If you own only one cat, you do not need any elaborate pharmaceutical supplies. Should your cat get seriously ill or have an accident, you will want to consult a veterinarian anyway.

You should never give a cat medications intended for humans because many of them are harmful for cats, and even if they are not, the wrong dosage is likely to produce negative effects. Also, many medicines are good only for a certain length of time; after that they may lose their effectiveness or turn poisonous. You should therefore be sure to throw away all medicines left over at the end of therapy prescribed by the veterinarian.

It does make sense to have a thermometer and a pair of tweezers on hand for your cat, and you will, of course, want to keep the medications prescribed by the veterinarian in a safe place (out of reach of children) for the course of the treatment.

Euthanasia

Cats have a long life expectancy and are likely, if cared for properly, to live happily and in good health for many years. Still, situations arise when a cat owner has to consider the question of euthanasia. If a cat loses all pleasure in life, or is in constant pain as a result of an accident or some chronic, incurable disease, or has become senile, many a cat owner will realize that it is in everybody's interest to terminate the animal's suffering.

Unlike humans, cats do not think about death, and it is possible to kill them in a way that causes them neither fear nor pain. Once a

Cat Diseases and How to Keep Your Cat Healthy

cat owner has come to the decision that the sick pet should suffer no longer, the veterinarian can put it to sleep gently by injecting a narcotic from which it will not wake again. Needless to say, the cat's human friend should be there to comfort the animal in this sad situation.

The Sexual Life of Cats and Raising Kittens

Neutering a Cat—Yes or No?

Although watching kittens grow up is delightful, you should seriously ask yourself, particularly if your cat is a purebred, whether you have the time, money, and knowledge necessary for breeding cats. Even in the case of an ordinary house cat, a responsible person should not simply let nature take its course. Just think what the consequences would be.

Let us assume that a cat has kittens twice a year and that only four of each litter survive, each of which then reproduces at the same rate. The result after ten years would be over 60 million cats.

These "unplanned" cats are likely to become strays, get sick, shot, or run over, or perish in some other sad manner. You can prevent this feline misery by having your cat neutered. I myself have five cats, all of them neutered, that enjoy a happy life summer and winter outside in the barn, shed, and yard. They do not go racing off madly after every rival or female in heat and are therefore exposed to much less danger than unneutered cats.

Unsupervised matings can also spread some of the most feared feline diseases (infectious peritonitis, leukemia, page 79) as well as parasites (fleas and mites, page 67).

Neutering Male and Female Cats

Neutering a cat usually means removing its reproductive organs by surgical process. In the male, the testicles are removed; in the female, the ovaries. Neutering is recommended for any cat that you do not intend to breed. The operation also disposes of the problems associated with sexual behavior (yowling and the odor of spraying), and it in no way diminishes the cat's enjoyment of life.

When the source of sexual hormones is eliminated, the need to satisfy sexual impulses disappears.

Ordinary female house cats usually reach sexual maturity at seven months, but in exceptional cases cats can become pregnant as early as five months. Male cats can fertilize females at about eight months of age. Siamese and Oriental cats tend to be sexually precocious, while long-haired males become sexually mature somewhat later.

Male cats should not be castrated before they reach sexual maturity—at about eight to ten months—because they may develop problems passing urine. Older males can be castrated at any time. The operation should be performed only by a veterinarian with the animal under anesthesia. After the hairs have been removed and the scrotum has been washed with an antiseptic, two small cuts are made to expose the testicles which are then severed carefully so that there is no severe bleeding or cause for infection.

Eight to ten months is also the minimum age at which a female cat can be spayed. The opinion that a cat should be allowed to have one litter of kittens before being spayed persists but has no scientific basis. It is true, however, that a cat should not be in heat at the time of the operation. A female cat can be spayed even after she has had a number of litters.

The spaying of a cat also has to be done with the animal anesthetized. The abdominal cavity is opened and the ovaries, usually with part of the uterus, removed. The operation requires a small incision that is visible on the outside. But there is no reason for excessive worry since most cats recover from the operation without any complications. Even cats that are already pregnant can be spayed, preferably as soon after the mating has occurred as possible. In this case, the entire uterus is removed with the ovaries (ovariohyster-ectomy).

Normally the operation required to neuter both male and female cats is quite simple, and the animals can be taken home immediately afterwards. With some commonly used anesthetics, the eyes of the cat remain open with enlarged pupils, and the breathing is slowed. The cat should be kept warm as long as it is under the effect of the drug, and it should not be fed at all until the anesthetic has completely worn off and the animal resumes its normal behavior.

In contrast to neutering or altering, sterilizing a cat means that the animal — male or female — is rendered infertile, without affecting the sexual impulses. In this operation, which is also performed under anesthesia, the hormone-producing sexual glands (testicles, ovaries) are left intact and merely the spermatic cords or the uterine tubes are cut or tied.

Since the sterilization of cats does not eliminate any of the behavior associated with feline sexuality that is unpleasant for the owners (spraying, yowling, restlessness, roaming, attempts to escape), castration or spaying are preferable, especially since, as I have already mentioned, these surgical procedures have no adverse effects on the animals.

Cats and "the Pill"

If you do not want your pedigreed cat to have kittens for a while but wish to breed her at some later time, you can resort to hormones to suppress the estrous cycle and reproduction. Hormones can be administered either as pills or as injections with long-term effectiveness. But extended hormone treatment, whether in the form of "the pill" or of injections, always carries with it a certain danger

of causing uterine problems such as infections of the uterus.

The Cat in Heat

A female cat comes into heat (is ready to mate) at certain times of the year depending on the climate. In temperate regions, early fall is such a time, and in southern regions, December and January. In Western Europe, the mating season for ordinary cats usually comes in February, June, and October. Purebred cats usually come in heat in February and then again in June. General rules cannot be given because individual cats and breeds vary.

Unlike female cats, tomcats can be sexually active at any time. Contrary to widespread opinion, mother cats can enter a new heat period and get pregnant again soon after giving birth and while still nursing a previous litter. One unpedigreed and not-yet-spayed cat I had came in heat and conceived nine days after having given birth.

An unspayed female will have two to three heat periods a year, each lasting three to six days. If no mating takes place, the heat continues for ten days and sometimes for as long as two or three weeks. If such a cat is not allowed contact with a male over a long period, hormonal disturbances may occur, resulting in permanent heat, false pregnancy, or uterine infection (pyometra).

In some breeds (for example, the Siamese), the symptoms of heat are particularly pronounced, causing sleepless nights and torment for both the human owner and the feline. The cat in heat eats less, keeps running around restlessly, meows, and rubs her head up against objects and the people she knows. The peak of the heat (usually the third day) is marked by loud yowling, and the cat writhes on the floor, usually close to "her" human.

The Sexual Life of Cats and Raising Kittens

She also keeps licking her paws and vulva. If you pet her along the back, she raises her rear high, crouches down in front, and keeps stepping from paw to paw with her hindlegs. These are clear signs of heat. If the cat's behavior is not as unambiguous as this, you can lightly tap the anal region with the flat of your hand. If the cat is in heat, she will inevitably raise her rear and start stepping in place with her hind feet.

Valuable pedigreed cats that the owner does not want to spay can either be given heat-suppressing medication ("anti-baby pills") or a hormone injection that is effective for at least three months and sometimes for six months or longer (page 84).

The Stud

It is practically impossible to keep a functioning tomcat in an apartment. The odor is unbearable, and the spraying leaves smelly, brownish spots on furniture and wallpaper. How and where can you then keep a stud? There are two possibilities: you can reserve a special room for him in the apartment, or you can keep him in a little house of his own outside. You can build the house yourself. It has to be so constructed that a bride can be accommodated in it comfortably at any time. It is cruel to keep a male cat all by himself, although I have unfortunately seen this done more than once. He should be given at least one companion (male or female), and this companion should be a cat he accepts and gets along with well.

Anyone wanting to breed a purebred female should not use just any stud in the neighborhood but carefully select the right individual for siring kittens. Associations of breeders of pedigreed cats print lists of studs in their publications. To qualify for listing, a male cat has to receive the predicate "excellent" in at least one exhibition every year, or he has to be an International Champion. The registry also requires a certificate of health and of vaccination by a veterinarian. A fee is often charged for inclusion in the list.

Courtship and Mating

An unneutered female cat that is allowed outside chooses her own mate, and she does not necessarily select the strongest or handsomest of her suitors. Quite often while two rivals for her affections fight over her, she makes off with a third.

A tomcat with no access to a receptive female will try to rape any female or young cat he finds, including even pregnant females and younger males. This is true, of course, only of cats that live indoors. Male cats that go outside generally find a female in heat, even if they have to travel several miles in pursuit. I have also observed "homosexual" activity in the stud I own; he mounts other males, preferably young ones, and drags them around.

Ordinary cats mate in the open, quite without inhibitions and without seeking cover. I have watched pairs mate right in the middle of our country road where there is quite a bit of traffic. Nor does the presence of people nearby distract them from their intention.

As I have already mentioned, you need to find a suitable partner for your pedigreed female. You can look for such an animal either in the stud registry of your cat association or at a cat show. Then you have to notify the owner of the stud of your choice in time, and make sure your cat's vaccination record is up to date. Often a statement from a veterinarian that your cat is free from leukemia (page 79) is also required. You should take

The Sexual Life of Cats and Raising Kittens

Mating. The tomcat climbs on top of the crouching female...grabs her by the scruff of her neck, and introduces the penis into her vagina.

your cat to the stud on the third day of her heat and leave her there two to three days until the mating has taken place.

The male cat usually indicates his readiness to mate by "spraying": he sprays a few drops of urine on some object while trembling with his tail. (Female cats also spray while in heat.) He conveys his "amorous intentions" to the beloved by yowling, licking his penis, and pacing restlessly in front of her. When he is actually ready to copulate, he tries to grab the female by the neck. If he misses, he sits down next to the writhing female and calls to her with a cooing sound. When he finally gets a hold of her, he mounts her (picture, above).

Soon after the introduction of the penis, the female begins to cry out while the male growls. The tip of the penis is barbed, but these barbs seem to have no function in the act of mating. Scientists found out that ovulation takes place and that the female emits her cry even when a smooth glass rod is inserted into the vagina.

When copulation is completed, the male usually leaps away quickly because the hissing female is likely to take a swipe at him with outstretched claws. She then rolls around violently a few times and licks her vulva. In contrast to many other kinds of animals, the act of copulation in cats triggers ovulation. If a female mates with two different males in the same heat period, ovulation takes place a second time, and two sets of ova with different genetic make-ups develop side by side. In other words, a single litter may contain kittens sired by different males.

Pregnancy

You cannot tell whether a mating was successful and the cat conceived until three weeks later. Then the teats, which are ordinarily a pale skin color, turn pink and become firmer and erect in a pregnant cat. The cat's overall shape does not change until about halfway through the pregnancy (after about thirty days) when the belly begins to get visibly rounder. During the last three weeks, you can see and feel the movements of the unborn kittens from the outside.

You can figure out the due date yourself. It is sixty-three days after the day of mating. Since pregnancy can vary between fifty-seven and seventy days in length, there is no reason to worry if the kittens are born up to seven days before or after the expected date.

By the twentieth day of pregnancy, the fer-

The Sexual Life of Cats and Raising Kittens

Unborn kittens (fetuses) in the womb. By the time they are born, they will be about 5 inches (13 cm) long.

tilized eggs have already grown to about 1/2 inch (10 millimeters). The fetus now grows an average of 1/8 inch (3 millimeters) per day, a little less at first and somewhat more toward the end, so that it measures about 5 inches (13 centimeters) at birth.

Make sure you offer your cat especially nutritious food during her pregnancy.

Most cats that live in close contact with people are especially affectionate and need especially loving care while they are pregnant. Often I have the feeling that my cat is trying to tell me quite specifically that it is time to get the maternity box ready. About two weeks before the kittens are expected, I set up the box so that the cat can get used to it. A solid cardboard box about 16 × 20 inches (40 × 50 centimeters) with sides about 12 inches (30 centimeters) high works fine. I line the box with a thick layer of newspapers which I cover with a clean cloth. The cats shows her approval by jumping into the box, bunching up the cloth, and kneading it while purring. This bed is placed in a quiet and warm spot and remains there until the kittens are ready to leave their mother.

Getting Ready for Kittens

After a gestation period of sixty to sixty-six, or occasionally fifty-seven to seventy days, the mother cat gives birth to one to eight (rarely more) kittens. Independent animals retreat to a protected spot to have their kittens while those that are close to their owners like to have their favorite person close by and accept assistance gladly. Cats that spend most of their time outdoors seek out a secluded place in a hay loft, an abandoned barn, a wood shed, or under bushes where they can give birth more or less undisturbed. These independent creatures then reappear only when their kittens are big enough to come trotting behind, tails raised high. Unfortunately, it is too late by then to have the unwanted kittens put to sleep easily, and it may be difficult to find homes for them. On farms they are often left to themselves and many of them die of sicknesses caused by malnutrition or infectious diseases against which they have not been vaccinated. The fate of such unwanted creatures is equally grim in cities, where they turn up as strays begging for food in cemeteries, parks, and parking lots. But, as I have said, tame house cats used to living with people tend to like human company when their time comes. If the litter is larger than anticipated or wished, the newborn kittens can be put to sleep painlessly by the veterinarian. But consider seriously whether it would not be a good idea to have the mother cat spayed later.

Delivery

Several days before the birth, the mother cat gets restless and keeps going to her maternity box. Shortly before the event is about to take place, she claws and rearranges her bed, lies down in it for a while, gets up again to visit the litter box without using it, and paces around restlessly. At this point I like to settle

The Sexual Life of Cats and Raising Kittens

This is how a mother cat transports her kitten: she grabs it gently but firmly by the scruff of the neck...

... which makes the kitten hang motionless and stiff so that it can be carried more easily.

down near the maternity box and talk softly to the cat, which, I am convinced, she appreciates. I stroke her belly gently, which gives me a chance to feel the unborn kittens move and to detect the first, usually light, contractions. The next thing that happens is that the water breaks. Soon after, the first kitten can be seen emerging, still enclosed in the amniotic sac (color photographs, page 92). Then it is pushed out with strong contractions. The mother carefully cleans the area around the vulva and, if the amniotic sac has not already burst, she bites it open and frees the kitten from it. After one or several more contractions the afterbirth is passed and usually eaten by the mother. This is done in part to clean up, but the afterbirth also has a lot of food value, and the cat is usually not hungry for a day or two after eating it. You therefore need not worry if a healthy mother cat refuses to eat after giving birth.

The mother also bites off the umbilical cord. Pedigreed cats sometimes neglect to do this, and it is then up to the human attendant to tear the cord. In order not to injure the newborn's abdomen, you should hold the cord close to the body and tear or pinch off the part that is away from the body. In this way you prevent bleeding, which is more likely to result from a smooth cut made with scissors.

Half an hour to an hour later, after some more contractions, the next kitten is born. The birth process thus stretches out over two to three hours, sometimes over a whole day. Kittens weigh between 2 and 4 ounces (60–130 grams) at birth.

If the cat is exhausted but the contractions continue without producing any more results, you have to call a veterinarian. In Persians it sometimes happens that a kitten gets stuck in the birth canal because of the breed's broad head or because it is lying in a cross position. Here the assistance of a veterinarian is mandatory.

After each kitten is born, the mother cat cleans it off while purring, and she is grateful if you bring a refreshing drink to her box after all the work she has done.

The Sexual Life of Cats and Raising Kittens

Raising Kittens

The First Few Days and Weeks

Kittens are born blind and deaf, but their sense of smell is already well developed. If you hold your finger up to their noses, they will start spitting on their very first day. Soon after having been licked clean, they will start nosing about for their mother's teats very purposefully.

As a rule, cats have eight teats, arranged in pairs. If there are more than six kittens in a litter, some of them may not get enough to eat. Even in smaller litters, there is always a wild scramble for the teats, a scramble in which each of the kittens tries to push its competitors out of the way with its paws. The kittens wrap their little tongues tightly around the teats and hold on almost continually for the first couple of days, even when they have stopped drinking and have fallen asleep. While nursing, the kittens knead to stimulate the flow of milk. The mother licks up the kittens' excreta and also massages their stomachs with her tongue.

When the kittens are two or three days old, the mother starts leaving them for short spells and later moves them—I have observed this in my own cats—to an entirely new place. To do this she grabs each kitten firmly by the neck, which causes it to hang there rigidly. She resorts to the same method of carrying when she returns a kitten that was accidentally dragged out of the box while hanging onto a teat.

The eyes of kittens open between the eighth and the eleventh day. At the same time the first teeth appear. In the fourth week the kittens begin to play, even though their movements are still quite awkward and clumsy. The incisor teeth come in between the fourth and the eighth week.

As soon as the kittens are able to get in and out of their next by themselves, you should set up a litter box for them. A plastic tub about 20 ¼ 24 inches (50 ¼ 60 centimeters) with sides about 2 inches (5 centimeters) high serves well and should be filled with about 1 inch (3 centimeters) of litter.

At this point the kittens still get plenty of nourishment through their mother's milk; but, at about four weeks, you can start offering them mushy and soft foods. Small kittens lick up baby cereal prepared with milk with great gusto (page 39).

Raising Kittens with a Substitute Mother

If everything goes normally, cats—whether pedigreed or not—raise their kittens without any problems for the first few weeks. The mother provides all the nourishment, and she has to get a diet particularly rich in vitamins and nutrients during this time. But if the kittens were delivered by Caesarean section, the mother sometimes does not have any milk. This can also happen because of hormonal disturbances. The easiest way to cope with this situation is to find a substitute mother or "wet-nurse." I kept track for forty days of the weight of two foster Persian kittens my Siamese mother cat raised along with her own litter. The results are shown in the accompanying table. It turned out that the two young Persians developed just as well along the norms of their breed as did their Siamese foster siblings; in other words, the Siamese wet-nurse looked after them with as much care as she gave to her own offspring. I shall never forget the cute picture the Siamese mother cat with her fuzzy Persian "babies" made.

Bottle-feeding Kittens

If you cannot find a nursing mother cat for your orphaned kittens, you have no choice but to bottle-feed them every two hours, day

The Sexual Life of Cats and Raising Kittens

and night. You also have to massage their little bellies and the bladder area gently with a tissue so that urine and feces will be passed, then rub some baby oil on the anal region. As a substitute for mother's milk I can recommend Borden's KMR. You should always have some formula milk and a doll-sized baby bottle with a nipple or a Pet-Nip® (available at pet stores) on hand whenever kittens are due.

Bottle feeding. This is how you hold the kitten to give it its bottle. (Both formula milk and bottles are available at pet stores.)

Weights of Kittens*

Day	Body weight in grams		Day	Body weight in grams	
Birth	120	115			
1	130	110	21	340	290
2	130	120	22	340	300
3	130	130	23	365	310
4	140	130	24	390	325
5	150	140	25	400	340
6	160	150	26	410	360
7	160	150	27	420	370
8	170	165	28	435	380
9	200	170	29	450	390
10	200	180	30	470	400
11	220	200	31	490	420
12	240	210	32	500	430
13	260	215	33	530	470
14	265	225	34	530	460
15	290	240	35	530	470
16	280	240	36	540	485
17	300	270	37	550	495
18	310	280	38	555	510
19	320	280	39	570	520
20	330	290	40	580	530

*Daily weights over forty days of two Persian kittens raised by a substitute mother (= male kitten;   = female kitten).

Young short-haired cats. ▷
Above: Six Burmese, lilac and chocolate, from the same litter.
Below: Blue Abyssinian with her three kittens.

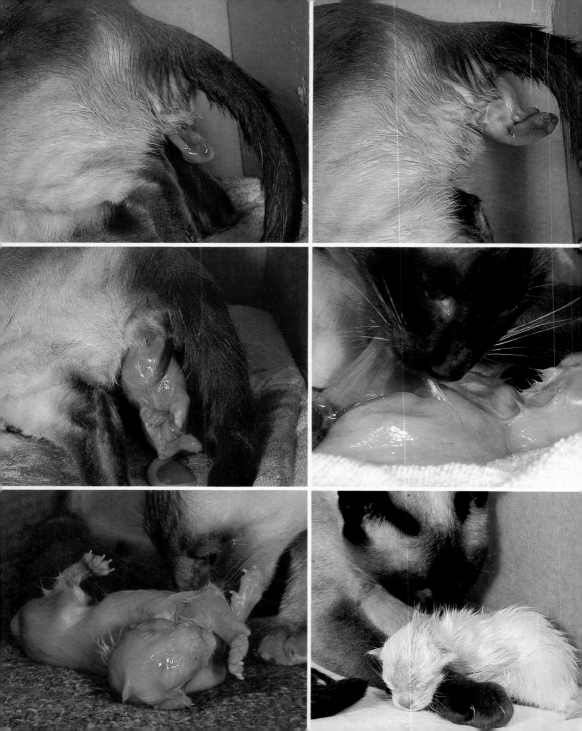

The Sexual Life of Cats and Raising Kittens

Giving Away Kittens

When the kittens are about twelve weeks old, they should make the transition to their new families. At this point they will have had their first shots and will be dewormed. Kittens that are taken away from their mothers too early show the negative effects of this premature separation for the rest of their lives.

It is not easy to find good homes for kittens, even if they are tame and used to people. We all have seen signs reading "Free kittens." This kind of advertisement may tempt irresponsible persons to take a kitten—it doesn't cost anything, after all—and keep it as long as it is fun. Later, when the animal requires some time or money, it is considered a burden and taken to an animal shelter or even simply abandoned somewhere. Sometimes pets that were acquired free are also sold later for money to people engaged in providing laboratory animals. So I urge you to give away kittens only to people you personally know to be reliable and truly fond of animals. A young cat which you have raised at the expense of time and effort as well as money should be valued enough by its new owner so that he or she does not mind paying for its food and vaccinations.

To find buyers for pedigreed kittens, you can advertise in pet magazines, publications of breeders' associations, or newspapers. Often the local chapter of your breeders' association can help to make contact with potential buyers.

While nursing, the kittens knead their mother's belly, which stimulates the milk flow.

◁ The birth of a cat. Above left: The kitten becomes visible in the birth canal. Above right: The contractions push the kitten out. Middle left: A breech birth. Middle right: The mother cat tears open the amniotic sac. Below left: Now she bites the umbilical cord and eats the afterbirth. Below right: The newborn kitten is licked dry by its mother.

Breeding Pedigreed Cats

Prerequisites

Kittens are pretty and cute; just about everyone enjoys watching them, and most cat owners would like to have the experience of seeing kittens born and raising them at least once.

But breeding pedigreed cats properly is not all that simple, and it is worthwhile to familiarize oneself with all the prerequisites and possible consequences before embarking on the venture.

Breeding cats presupposes not only a love for animals but also idealism, and knowledge of the special needs of the animals, adequate space, and lots of time.

Even if you have only one cat you wish to breed, you should have a special, quiet room where she can give birth and nurse the kittens and where up to eight kittens can grow up without your having to worry that they might get into trouble or do damage to anything.

You have to be a member of a cat club if you want to have official pedigrees for your kittens. The stud fee for a good Champion or International Champion male runs from about 50 to 300 dollars, to which you have to add travel time and expenses (taking your cat to the stud and picking her up). But keeping a stud is even more expensive and troublesome than keeping a female (just think of the problem of odor) if the animal is to live a decent life (page 85). The birth of pedigreed kittens involves complications (page 87) more often than that of ordinary kittens so that you may have to pay veterinarian's bills. In short, you are not likely to make money raising pedigreed cats, and finding good homes for the young animals can be discouraging. How can you be sure if the animal will be well-treated? There are already pedigreed cats in animal shelters, and the supply in many breeds exceeds the demand, at least at times.

Another essential for breeding pedigreed cats is a thorough understanding of the principles of genetics.

Goals of Breeding

The minimum goal of breeding is to produce physically and psychologically healthy animals. Beyond this, the breeder may attempt to improve the strain of his animals and come closer to the ideal of the breed as he conceives of it or as prescribed by the official standard. Under certain conditions it is also possible to develop new breeds (page 102) or color variations.

Producing beautiful kittens of recognized breeds requires knowledge, persistence, time, money, and luck. Thoughtlessly increasing the number of pedigreed cats in the hope of selling the kittens at a profit generally results only in swelling the number of miserable unwanted animals. There are also breeders who are so singlemindedly intent on winning first prizes with their animals at cat shows that affection for the individual cat becomes secondary or nonexistent, and the owners dispose of the cats that do not achieve the anticipated success.

Choosing pedigreed parents of the right color is important in trying to produce kittens of superior quality, and I have drawn up a table of desirable, undesirable, and impossible combinations of parents as an aid to breeders of pedigreed cats.

Breeding Pedigreed Cats

Color Combinations for Mating Pedigreed Cats*

	White (pure breed)	Black Blue Red Cream	Black smoke Blue smoke	Silver tabby	Brown tabby	Red tabby	Chinchilla	Cameo	Blue cream	Tortoiseshell Blue tortoiseshell	Tortoiseshell with white Blue tortoiseshell with white	Bi-color	Colorpoint	Birman
White (pure breed)	O	O							O	O			O	
Black Blue Red Cream	O	O	O						O	O	O	O	O	
Black smoke Blue smoke		O	O						O	O				
Silver tabby				O										
Brown tabby					O									
Red tabby						O								
Chinchilla							O							
Cameo								O						
Blue cream	O	O	O						ø	ø	ø	O	O	
Tortoiseshell Blue tortoiseshell	O	O	O						ø	ø	ø	O	O	
Tortoiseshell with white Blue tortoiseshell with white		O							ø	ø	ø	O		
Bi-color		O							O	O	O	O		
Colorpoint		O							O	O			O	
Birman														O

*Explanation of symbols: O ½ desirable combination; blank ½ undesirable combination;
ø ½ impossible because found only in females.

95

Breeding Pedigreed Cats

The following introduction to genetics as it applies to cats is not to be used as a set of directions for breeding cats. It is meant only to give you a glimpse of the complexities of genetics and to stimulate your interest in this huge and interesting field. Our goal is not to have more and more cats in the world, but to have better ones.

How Can Cat Clubs Help Out?

A cat club unites keepers, breeders, and lovers of all kinds of cats and represents their interests by promoting the purity of breeds and optimal conditions for keeping cats as pets.

The clubs try to achieve these goals by bringing together breeders and fanciers of pedigreed cats; providing a forum for breeders to share their experiences at meetings and in specialized publications; organizing scientific lectures; offering theoretical and practical information on all aspects of breeding, genetics, care, nutrition, and standards for judging cats; organizing cat exhibitions; keeping a registry of pedigreed cats and issuing pedigrees; and training cat breeders to become judges.

In the United States, the Cat Fanciers' Association (CFA) is the largest cat association, and in Great Britain the Governing Council of the Cat Fancy (GCCF) is the central organization of cat clubs. Both these bodies work together with Fédération Internationale Féline (FIFe), keep in close contact, exchange judges and try to establish worldwide breed standards. FIFe, founded in Paris in 1949, represents associations from many countries in Europe, Asia, the Americas, and Australia.

Serious cat clubs have strict guidelines they expect their members to adhere to. I should like to list here some of the most important rules, rules drawn up to protect the cats:
• Female cats may not be bred before they are one year old; exceptions require special permission by a veterinarian.
• At least three months must elapse before a second litter, and no more than two litters per year are permitted.
• The mating of siblings and the crossing of breeds is allowed only with the special permission of the club's breeding committee.
• A report of the kittens' birth has to be sent within four weeks of the event to the cat association's central office, which will then issue pedigrees.
Equally stringent rules apply to male cats listed in the stud registry. Kittens may be transferred to a new owner only if they are properly vaccinated, are at least twelve weeks old, and will not be resold.

Reproduction and Heredity

Many characteristics, or traits, that members of a species share or that distinguish them from each other are inherited, passed on from parent to offspring in the genes. Not all mechanisms of heredity are fully explored, but most of the principles are understood.

When fertilization occurs, two germ cells unite: a *sperm cell* from the male enters the *egg cell* of the female. All living beings are made up of cells, each of which consists of cell plasma and a cell nucleus. The nucleus is essential for the vital functions of the cell, and it is in the nucleus that the *chromosomes,* which carry the genetic information, are found. The chromosomes are arranged in pairs with one half of the pair coming from the father and the other from the mother.

The *division of the cell nucleus* forms the basis of the multiplication of cells, of growth, and of reproduction and inheritance. Sexual reproduction requires a special kind of cell division so that in the process of fertilization the number of chromosomes in the cells of the new creature remains the same from one generation to the next.

The normal division of somatic cells (mitosis) always produces two new cells with a constant number of double, or diploid, chromosomes. However, in the division of cells called meiosis, which is characteristic of sexual reproduction, cells with only one chromosome of each type, with only one half of the normal chromosome number (haploid number), are created. In the process of fertilization, when the egg cell unites with the sperm cell, two haploid chromosome sets combine to make up the normal diploid number again in the fertilized egg, or zygote, from which the new organism grows.

Each species of creature has its own predetermined number of chromosomes. Cats have thirty-eight chromosomes, or nineteen chromosome pairs. Only animals with the same chromosome number can mate. This is why it is impossible, for instance, to cross rabbits with hares.

Apart from the chromosomes that carry general genetic information, there is a pair of chromosomes that determines sex. These chromosomes have the shape of either an X or a Y. In mammals, the presence of two X chromosomes produces a female, and the combination of one X and one Y results in a male.

Remember: female = XX; male = XY.

Genes are located in pairs on the two complementary chromosomes inside the cell nucleus. All the genes taken together represent the totality of inherited factors, also called the *genotype.* This determines to a large extent what a cat looks like. The individual genes are reproduced and can change. A change in genes is called a *mutation.* Mutations happen spontaneously and are an important factor in the gradual change of species in the course of evolution. Only those mutations that do not represent a serious disadvantage to the viability of the organism survive over an extended time period. If a mutation brings advantages to the organism, then it can spread throughout the species in the course of many generations and eventually replace the old genotype altogether.

If people follow the principles of selective breeding in choosing mates for their cats, they can make use of desirable mutations and create a new breed in a relatively short time. Well-known gene mutations in cats are long hair, the curly fur of Rex cats, and the dark points of Siamese cats.

I have listed some important hereditary factors of house cats in the table below. In each case there is a wild form which is usually *dominant* and therefore prevalent. The change in the original hereditary material of the wild form, the mutant, is usually *recessive,* which means that the trait is less likely to appear in the animals and is therefore "hidden."

Internationally accepted abbreviations for the various genetic factors have been introduced to simplify the representation of genetic processes, breeding programs, and experimental matings. Capital letters indicate dominant traits, and lower case letters, recessive ones.

Breeding Pedigreed Cats

Some Important Genes of House Cats

Wild form		Mutant		Wild form		Mutant	
Symbol*	Name	Symbol*	Name	Symbol*	Name	Symbol*	Name
A	Agouti or natural coloring (banded hairs)	a	Non-agouti; hairs are uni-colored rather than banded	m	Normal tail	M	Manx tail, shorter than normal
B	Basic black coloring	b	Brown or choco-late colored,	o	Normal colors, no red	O	Orange (sex-linked)
		b^l	Light brown	pd	Normal number of toes	p	Pink-eyed dilute
C	Unicolored	c^{ch}	Silver			Pd	Polydactylism; having more than the normal number of toes
		c^b	Burmese				
		c^s	Siamese				
		c^a	Blue-eyed albino	R	Normal, smooth hair	r	Cornish Rex hair, curly
		c	Pink-eyed albino			re	Devon Rex hair
D	Undiluted color	d	Blue dilution	s	Normal coat color without white patches	S	Color interspersed with white spots or patches (Pie-bald White Spotting)
fd	Normal, pointed ears	Fd	Folded ears				
Hr	Normal, full coat	h	Hairlessness				
i	Fur colored all over	I	Inhibitor: part of the hair is not colored (colored points or tipping)	T	Tabby pattern (mackerel)	T^a t^b	Abyssinian tabby Blotched tabby, classic pattern of patches or stripes
L	Normal hair, short hair	l	Long hair, longer than normal	w	Normal coat color	W	White coat (Dominant White)
						Wh	Wirehair

*Capital letter = dominant gene; lowercase letter = recessive gene.

Breeding Pedigreed Cats

Unicolor, for example, is represented by the letter C, whereas "d" means "dilution," a muting of the color intensity caused by the so-called "dilution gene" (black is diluted into blue, red into cream). The gene for pink-eyed albinism (c) causes the hereditary absence of pigments in the skin, the hair, and the eyes. It is always recessive and can be observed in almost all animals and in humans.

Heredity works by the passing on of genes from parents to their offspring, and this happens according to definite laws known as Mendel's laws.

Mendel's Laws

Attempts to cross different strains of animals and plants were made as early as the eighteenth century. But Johann Gregor Mendel, an Austrian monk who lived from 1822 to 1884, was the first to investigate systematically how inherited traits are passed on. He found out in the process of his research that different patterns of inheritance recur with statistically predictable consistency. This discovery and the laws deduced from it form the basis of genetics.

Mendel's first law. If two pure strains, differing only in one trait for which one parent carries two dominant genes and the other two recessive genes, are crossed, all the offspring of the first generation will *look alike* in respect to this trait.

The *dominant* gene is displayed in this first crossing, whereas the *recessive* is not. It does not matter which gene is carried by the father and which by the mother. If we cross, for instance, a male cat with two genes for a black coat and a female with two genes for a blue coat, the kittens will have genes for both black and blue; but since black is dominant

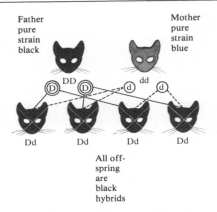

Illustration of Mendel's First Law. If a male cat with a pure strain for black coat color (DD) is mated with a female with a pure strain for blue (dd), all resulting kittens have genes from both their parents, one black and one blue gene (Dd). They look black because the color black is dominant.

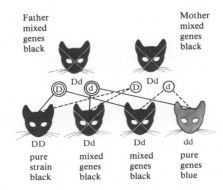

Illustration of Mendel's Second Law. If first-generation hybrids with one gene for black and one for blue (Dd) are mated, the gene pattern for color in the next generation exhibits the ratio 1:2:1 — pure strain black (DD) once; mixed genes black (Dd) twice; and pure strain blue (dd) once.

99

Breeding Pedigreed Cats

and blue recessive, all the kittens will be black.

The products of such a crossing of different strains are called *hybrids*. They are monohybrids, since the parents differ in only one trait, color. There are also dihybrids (with mixed gene pairs for two traits) and polyhybrids (with mixed gene pairs for several traits).

Mendel's second law. If hybrids of the first generation are crossed with each other, their offspring will *not look alike*. Instead, the characteristics of both grandparents reappear in some of the grandchildren in homozygous form (i.e., both genes are the same). In monohybrids the ratio is always 1 : 2 : 1. In our example of black and blue cats, for instance, the resulting third generation would have the following genetic ratio: one black cat with 2 black genes (DD); two black cats with 1 black and 1 blue gene (Dd); and one blue cat with 2 blue genes (dd).

There are also traits for which neither gene is dominant or recessive and where the crossing of two strains produces a "mixture." In the flower Japanese four-o'clock, for instance, the crossing of plants bearing red flowers and others bearing white ones results in pink four o'clocks.

Backcrossing. In the case of a black male cat it is impossible to know, even if he has a pedigree, whether he is a hybrid or whether his strain for black color is pure. We can only guess what genotype he is. There is no way of telling by looking at a black cat whether or not the potential for blue color is hidden in his genes. If we want to find out for sure, we can do so by backcrossing.

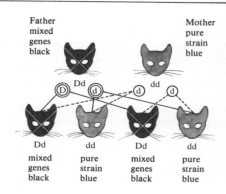

Backcrossing. If a black male cat with mixed genes (Dd) is mated with a female of pure blue strain (dd), the ratio of the offspring is 1:1, so there are as many black kittens with mixed genes (Dd) as there are pure strain blue ones (dd).

We do this by mating him with a female that we know has the blue factor. This should be a blue cat with two genes for blue color (a blue-black cat has only one blue gene). If the black male is a hybrid, the ratio of the offspring will be 1:1, so that there will be the same number of blue homozygous kittens with two recessive blue genes (bb) as of heterozygous ones (Bb) which look like the dominant parent, which is, in our case, black.

This ratio reflects only a statistical reality; it can be expected to turn up consistently only in large samples. In a single litter of four kittens all of them might be black by sheer chance, and we cannot decide with certainty whether or not the father has a gene for blue. But if even one of the kittens is blue, we know for a fact that the father contributed a blue gene. As the number of kittens increases and no blue ones show up, the probability increases that the father is of a pure black strain.

Breeding Pedigreed Cats

Phenotype

The phenotype, or the appearance of a creature, is a result of the combined effects of inheritance and environment. Appearance can be particularly deceptive when it is a question of genetic makeup.

White fur color is a good example of this. White fur color (not the rare albino white) is dominant over every other color and pattern of marking. This means that a white cat may have the potential in its genes for any other color. There are, of course, some pure strains of white which, when paired with any color cat, will always produce white offspring. But most white cats are heterozygous. Such a cat is like a "grab bag," and when a pair of them get together it is anybody's guess what colors will turn up in the litter.

Gene Coupling — Sex-Linked Inheritance

Hemophilia, a disorder affecting the blood in humans, has achieved notoriety, in part because it has affected members of European royalty. In this disease the clotting of the blood is impaired, and so-called "bleeders" can bleed to death as a result of even the slightest wound. This disease affects only men, and the predisposition for it is linked to the sex chromosome.

A comparable phenomenon found in cats is the sex-linked inheritance of the color red. If a female cat has a gene for red color on both X chromosomes (page 97), she will be all red. If she has a red gene on one of the X chromosomes and, say, black on the other, she will have black fur with red patches (tortoiseshell). Male cats have, as we know, only one X chromosome. If the color gene on it is for red, the cat will always be red because there is no second X chromosome that could carry

For the first four weeks, kittens get all their nourishment from their mother's milk. Afterwards they can be given some mushy or soft food.

genetic information for tortoiseshell coloring. A male tortoiseshell cat is a great rarity and has the abnormal chromosome combination of XXY (Klinefelter Syndrome).

The phenomenon of sex-linked characteristics is responsible for the fact that the pairing of a black male with a red female produces different results from the pairing of a red male with a black female. By consulting the table on page 103 you can find out what color kittens to expect if you mate black, blue, red, tortoiseshell, cream, and blue cream cats. The pattern of inheritance of the color red is only one of many examples of linked genes.

Deafness in white Persians is also the result of linked genes. Deafness and blue eye color are genetically linked, but there are other contributing factors that also play a role in causing deafness in blue-eyed, white Persians. Breeders are not allowed to use cats with this defect as breeding stock because the deafness is passed on to the offspring, though sometimes in the hidden form of recessive genes. Not all the resulting kittens would necessarily be deaf, but all of them would have a hereditary predisposition for deafness.

Breeding Pedigreed Cats

Tailless Manx cats (page 129) exhibit another example of gene coupling. The dominant gene for taillessness (M) is linked to a lethal factor. If two tailless cats (both animals carry the lethal factor) are mated, all the homozygous offspring will die, usually before they are even born, because they have inherited a gene carrying the lethal factor from each of their parents. The lethal factor in Manx cats becomes evident, then, not so much in kittens that die after birth but in the small number of live-born kittens (usually one to three per litter).

Inbreeding

The mating of related individuals is called inbreeding. The closer the relationship between the two parents is, the higher the degree of inbreeding. The pairing of siblings is called incest breeding, and it represents the highest degree of inbreeding.

In inbreeding the genes present in the breeding stock keep being recombined without any new genes from different animals being added to the gene pool. This means that the genetic makeup of the inbred offspring is to a large extent the same, and the animals resemble each other more and more with each generation.

If the parents have recessive genes for negative traits, inbreeding will produce more and more animals that have inherited these genes from both sides. When recessive genes are inherited from both sides, there is no dominant gene to suppress the negative trait, and this negative trait becomes manifest in the appearance, or phenotype, of the animal, so that the defects of inbreeding become apparent. When defects of inbreeding show up, no more pairings of that type should be undertaken.

Conversely, inbreeding can produce more animals that have inherited a desirable trait from their two related parents. In this way inbreeding with genetically healthy animals can serve to establish and spread desired characteristics. But fanciers with little experience in breeding cats are not advised to choose a related partner for their cats.

Genetic Defects and Inherited Diseases

A genetic defect is a predisposition for a negative trait that is passed on from one generation to the next. Examples of genetic defects in cats are overbite, tearing eyes caused by nasal passages that are too narrow, bent tail, monorchidism (only one testicle is descended into the scrotum), predisposition for pyometra, sterility, gingivitis, etc.

It is important, therefore, to look over carefully any animals you intend to breed. This includes the strange stud. The fact that he may have won many prizes is not the decisive factor that makes him an excellent stud. What counts is the quality of his offspring. If the kittens he has sired look healthy and conform to their type, then he is a good candidate. At cat shows you will often have an opportunity to examine two or three generations of a line of breeding.

The Origin of a New Breed

A new breed can come into being either through a mutation or through a new combination of genes achieved by planned breeding. The original ancestor of a new breed may be a mutant that was the result of a chance mating.

Let me illustrate how a new breed can originate by drawing up a scenario involving

Breeding Pedigreed Cats

Inheritance of Coat Colors Black, Blue, Red, and Cream in Cats*

	Male kittens					Female kittens			
	Black father	**Blue father**	Red father	Cream father		Black father	**Blue father**	Red father	Cream father
Black mother	Black Blue	Black Blue	Black Blue	Black Blue	Black mother	Black Blue	Black Blue	Tortoise-shell Blue-cream	Tortoise-shell Blue-cream
Blue mother	Black Blue	Blue	Black Blue	Blue	Blue mother	Black Blue	Blue	Tortoise-shell Blue-cream	Blue-cream
Red mother	Red Cream	Red Cream	Red Cream	Red Cream	Red mother	Tortoise-shell Blue-cream	Tortoise-shell Blue-cream	Red Cream	Red Cream
Tortoise-shell mother	Black Blue Red Cream	Black Blue Red Cream	Black Blue Red Cream	Black Blue Red Cream	Tortoise-shell mother	Black Blue Tortoise-shell Blue-cream	Black Blue Tortoise-shell Blue-cream	Red Cream Tortoise-shell Blue-cream	Red Cream Tortoise-shell Blue-cream
Cream mother	Red Cream	**Cream**	Red Cream	Cream	**Cream mother**	Tortoise-shell Blue-cream	**Blue-cream**	Red Cream	Cream
Blue-cream mother	Black Blue Red Cream	Blue Cream	Black Blue Red Cream	Blue Cream	Blue-cream mother	Black Blue Tortoise-shell Blue-cream	Blue Blue-cream	Red Cream Tortoise-shell Blue-cream	Cream Blue-cream

*Example: A blue male cat and a cream female cat will produce only male cream and female blue-cream kittens.

103

Himalayan or Colorpoint Longhairs (page 120), a fairly new breed with the coloring of a Siamese and the long fur and the build of a Persian.

Let us assume that the owner of a black Persian has agreed to board a Siamese whose owner is away on vacation. Now let us further assume that what was not supposed to happen does happen: the Siamese male and the Persian female mate. The result of this misalliance is a litter of lovely black kittens exhibiting the dominant traits of their parents: all of them are black (the Persian heritage) and short-haired (the Siamese heritage). These kittens are, as we have learned above, hybrids with recessive genes for long hair and for Siamese coloring. If these cats are now allowed to mate with each other, chances are 1:15 that one of the offspring will be long-haired with Siamese coloring. A long shot, but possible!

If you are familiar with all the ins and outs of genetic laws and cross Persians and Siamese intentionally, you are then engaging in "planned breeding."

Cat Shows — Show Cats

Having served as a judge of pedigreed cats for years at international exhibitions, I would like to tell you a little about what goes on at these events. I would also like to tell you what you have to do to prepare for showing your cat.

Cats have been exhibited since the sixteenth century, but the first show that is at all comparable to our modern ones took place in London in 1871. Modern cat shows are pretty much the same all over the world. Even in Australia, where I once spent several weeks judging cats, I immediately felt at home as soon as I entered the exhibition hall.

Almost all shows last two days, though there are some national ones that take only one day. Cat shows are usually planned for weekends, and they are held throughout the year, though less frequently in the summer months of June to August. The most prestigious shows in the United States are held between the months of September and February. Depending on the size of the hall, anywhere from 200 to 1,000 cats of all breeds may be shown. There are also some specialized exhibitions that show, for instance, only Persians or only Siamese cats.

Entering a Show

If you intend to go in for breeding and showing cats, it is a good idea to join a club and get to know members with similar interests. A club will hold cat shows, and a specific breed club will also look after the general interests of the breed.

When you have decided to enter a show, write to the secretary of your club, asking for an entry form. This form must be filled out properly: in the case of a show affiliated with the Cat Fanciers' Association (CFA), for instance, the class in which the cat is to be entered must be given. This form should generally be sent in about six weeks before the date of the exhibition.

Eligibility

It may come as a surprise to you, but many cat clubs do not require that your cat have a pedigree. A well-cared-for and well-groomed common house cat is just as eligible to participate in a show of stars as the offspring of crossbreeding that cannot be assigned to a specific breed. Of course, any cat entering a show must have a sleek and silky coat.

To be eligible for entry, a cat must be registered with the organization sponsoring the show. More often than not, this organization is the CFA. Founded in 1906, the CFA is by far the largest registering body in the United States, with more than 575 member clubs, and is responsible for more than half the vast number of shows in this country. It held its first two impressive shows in 1906: one in Buffalo and one in Detroit. Although the CFA has no individual memberships, all members of locally affiliated cat clubs become associated automatically.

However, the great size of the United States makes it impractical to have only one body registering cats and sponsoring shows, so others were established. Among them are the Cat Fanciers' Federation (CFF), founded in 1919; the United Cat Federation (UCF) in 1946; the American Cat Fanciers' Association (ACFA) in 1955; and the Crown Cat Fanciers' Federation (CCFF) in 1965. The Canadian Cat Association (1961) is exclusively Canadian, but several of the other associations hold shows in both the United States and Canada, and the CFA is also associated with certain shows in Japan.

Several of the federations have banded together as the International Cat Association. They accept cats registered with any association at their shows, an arrangement that helps exhibitors considerably: otherwise, their cats would have to be registered with the specific organization running each show they wish to enter.

In addition to having the proper registration, a cat being entered in a show must be healthy, properly vaccinated, free of parasites, and not visibly pregnant. Sound health is obviously important, not only for your cat, but for the sake of all the other cats in the show. According to CFA rules, any cat from a house or cattery where there has been any fungus, or infectious or contagious illness within twenty-one days of the opening date of the show is ineligible and may not enter the showroom.

Other CFA rules require that kittens be at least four months old on the day a show opens; that each cat be entered in the breed under which it is registered; that altered cats be entered only in Premiership or Household Pet classes; and that a cat must have all its physical properties (eyes, ears, legs, claws, or tail if it is not a Manx). Once your cat has completed the requirements for Championship or Premiership status, it may not compete again until after the claim has been filed.

Aside from competition, kittens and cats may be entered in a show simply for exhibition or for sale. However, they may not appear at more than one show a week, and no more than two kittens or one cat may be kept in a single cage at the show.

Getting Ready for the Exhibition

Choose exhibitions held not too far from your home for your first contact with the world of cat shows, and make your first few visits without your cat so you have a chance to take everything in without distractions. I would not recommend taking your cat abroad for a show until you have had fairly extensive experience with exhibitions. This applies particularly if you do not speak the language of the host country.

A few weeks before the event you should also check to make sure your cat's vaccinations are up to date, sew some curtains for the exhibition cage — three curtains measuring 28 × 28 inches (70 × 70 centimeters), reserve a room in a hotel that permits pets (make sure the room has a bath if you are taking a male cat), and perhaps arrange for car pooling.

Two days before the show, clip the cat's claws. The day before the trip you should collect the following items: vaccination certificate, proof of identity for yourself, application papers, curtains and a small litter box for the exhibition cage, a larger litter box for use in the hotel, cat litter, garden trowel, two food dishes, cat food, powder (if you have a long-haired cat), comb, brush, and a plastic bag for dirty litter.

In preparation for the big event you may also want to test your cat's exhibition behavior. Place the cat in a carrier and ask someone not familiar with your cat but used to handling cats to take your cat out of the carrier and carry it around the house. It is even better if you can practice this in surroundings that are new to the cat. It will give you some indication of how the cat is likely to behave at the exhibition. Of course, the cat may react in completely different ways there because all the smells and sounds will be so unfamiliar. You should run through this routine in any event, particularly if the animal is young, so your cat has a chance to get used to the exhibition atmosphere. It is also advisable to get a cat used to traveling in a car at an early age (page 30).

Cat Shows — Show Cats

Staying in a Hotel

Before you release your cat from its carrier in a hotel room, make sure that all the windows are closed and that there are no inaccessible hiding places.

It can be a real tragedy if the cat disappears into an open ventilation shaft, to emerge again only after hours of coaxing and covered from head to tail with grime and dirt. A session of bathing, blow drying, and powdering is then unavoidable, and your night's rest may be ruined.

What Happens at the Exhibition

Vetting
Many shows require that each cat be examined by a veterinarian on arrival, before it is admitted to the showroom. The veterinarian carefully checks the mouth, ears, and anal region; feels the abdomen and lymph nodes; and looks over the whole animal for parasites. Any cat that shows evidence of fungus, fleas, ear mites, or any contagious or infectious disease is immediately disqualified. All healthy animals—generally the vast majority—are issued cards to that effect and may be put in their numbered cages in the showroom.

Other shows have veterinarian inspections only after someone—an exhibitor, judge, or show committee member—voices a suspicion that a certain cat is ill. The cat is then removed from the show room until the veterinarian can examine it. If the cat is suffering from a contagious or infectious illness, it is disqualified from any further competition in that show, although it does get to keep any prizes it has already won.

In the Showroom
When you arrive in the show-hall, one of the officials will hand you a card on which your name, your cat's name and the number of its cage is typed. You will also get a schedule of the various classes, the names of the judges (usually four), and their location in the show-hall.

As soon as your cat is examined and approved by a veterinarian (in case a veterinarian is assigned to the show), and safely placed in its show-cage, it is advisable to purchase a catalogue, so you will know who your competitors are.

Once you know that your cat is comfortable, it is time to locate the place where your cat will be judged. This place, the "ring," is a large table with a small platform, and behind it is the judge. On either side, behind the judge and arranged in a U, are about ten cages in which the cats will be placed by a steward prior to judging. At one side of that same table sits a clerk who keeps the records, enters your name and checks all the information against the notes in the catalogue.

The judge has a looseleaf notebook in which all entries are properly recorded. Each class is called on the loudspeaker and the cats placed in the cages behind the judge. These cages have the numbers of the corresponding cats attached to the front.

When all cats are ready to be judged, the judge will begin his examination. Each cat will be taken out of the cage—by the judge or the steward—and placed on the little platform in the center of the table, the "ring." A thorough examination follows. After each examination the judge disinfects his or her hands and the table. The final decision is reached by comparison and point evaluation against the breed standard. Then the ribbons are awarded, and the cats are retrieved by their proud (or disappointed) owners or agents.

Four to six winner's ribbons, with minimum scores, are needed for a cat to become a Champion in a single day. An agreed number of final wins can earn the title of Grand Champion, provided the judging was done by different judges.

Then the cages behind the judge's table are disinfected, and a new group of anxious cat owners is called. It goes without saying that the decision of the judge is always and inevitably final.

After the Show

Please do not be crushed if your cat does not rank among the winners and perhaps fails to get even an "excellent." Stay calm and do not lose your sense of humor. Perhaps you will do better next time. It always makes me very sad when I stroll through the exhibition hall on the second day of the show and see a cage with a "For Sale" sign that was not there the day before. Exciting as it is to drive home with a cat that has won a prize, we should always keep in mind that excessive ambition can be destructive to the love for our animals.

White Persian with blue eyes.   ▷

House Cats and Pedigreed Cats

House Cats

The first house cats probably evolved from some tawny colored animals that lived at the time of the Egyptians as early as the sixteenth century B.C. and took to domestication only reluctantly. Mice and rats were running rampant in the Egyptian granaries, where they found ideal living conditions, so the cats moved in. The hunting could hardly have been better.

People not only tolerated these predators that hunted rodents but welcomed and protected them. In this situation, the more trusting animals had a clear advantage over the shyer ones, who withdrew whenever people appeared. The trusting ones not only throve better in the custody of humans but were also able to have and raise more litters. Under these conditions, mutations in body structure, behavior, or coloring — changes that often lead to extinction sooner or later in wild populations — had a better chance to persist and spread. Even today, there are strains of cats that have developed their differences in response to various environmental conditions or human preferences. Variations in coat color and special physical traits — short and sturdy bodies versus long, svelte ones; heavy-set, square heads versus slim and narrow skulls — occur in house cats without human interference in the reproductive behavior of cats. But if people favor and encourage certain shapes and colors, then this has a definite, quantitative effect on the frequency with which these traits appear in the cat population.

Different breeds come into being when humans pair specific animals with the goal of creating future cat generations that reflect people's ideals. Even though many of today's cat breeds have exotic names and are said to go back to some not-always-correct geographic origin, all cats are ultimately descended from one and the same population. Their special traits were created through selection and knowledgeable pairing.

◁ Persians. Above left: Red Persian.
Above right: Bi-color Persian, black and white.
Middle left: Blue Persian. Middle right: Black Smoke Persian. Below left: Himalayan Red-point. Below right: Chinchilla Persian.

Cats that have moved away from human settlements, often because of overpopulation (too many cats in too small an area), and have to find their own food and fend for themselves much as wild animals do, quickly change back to the type favored by natural selection. Gray tigers (wild or agouti coloring) and black cats are generally more successful hunters and can evade enemies (including human hunters, dogs, foxes, owls, and eagles) more easily than multicolored cats or cats with white splotches, and therefore tend to live longer.

The Norwegian Forest Cat (page 122) is a typical example of what natural selection and the adaptability of the species produce. In the cold and wet climate where these cats live, a thick, long winter coat is extremely useful, and consequently the Norwegian Forest Cat has developed long, thick fur. In other geographical areas, it seems that small and delicate cats had an advantage over larger ones because they required less food and were thus able to multiply more.

House cats that forage for their own food feed almost exclusively on mice. Examination of stray cats that were shot (about 200,000 animals per year in the Federal Republic of Germany) proved this conclusively: about 90 percent of their stomach contents consisted of mice.

The opinion — still widely held in rural areas — that cats kept to get rid of mice should not be fed or should be fed only sparingly is wrong. Since the instinct to hunt and kill prey is considerably stronger than the desire to still hunger, well-fed (but not overfed), healthy, and strong cats are especially passionate hunters. Nor do cats present a serious threat to birds. The decrease in the variety of small birds that is taking place in many areas is more attributable to the destruction of the birds' habitats. The true reasons for the disappearance of many of our birds are the reduction or elimination of their feeding and nesting grounds and the build-up of environmental poisons in their food chain. Most cats succeed very rarely — and only when their luck is good — in catching healthy, adult birds.

In the course of their long history of living with mankind, cats have been valued very differently by different peoples. At the height of Egyptian civilization, when they first started living close to humans, they were not only appreciated but at

House Cats and Pedigreed Cats

times even revered as divine beings. The moon goddess Bubastis, for instance, was depicted with a cat's head.

The first cats that were introduced into Europe also enjoyed high regard. But cats later acquired a bad reputation when they, along with other small animals, were suspected of being the demonic "familiars" of witches, and were executed along with their owners.

Another superstition survived in some places long past the Dark Ages: live cats were mortared into the foundation walls of buildings to ensure the structure's permanence and to bring good luck to the inhabitants.

Cats were also associated with the love lives and the deaths of humans. The actions of cats or the relationships between people and cats were said to have prophetic meaning. Thus it was seen as a great misfortune if a cat died inside the house of its owner. And the medieval custom of stuffing an adulteress together with her cat into a sack and murdering both together is said to still have been practiced in the Near East in the last century.

Even today some people believe that seeing cats, especially black ones, is a bad omen. But most modern people associate good rather than bad luck with cats and love them as pets.

The Origin of a Breed

With cats — as with many other kinds of domestic animals — people have used selective breeding to create different variations of the basic form *(Felis silvestris)* and establish them as separate breeds. There is no need to consider productiveness or other traits for human usefulness as breeding criteria, and breeders are thus able to follow esthetic and emotional considerations in the selection of individuals for breeding. Incentives for breeding are, for example, a delight in the natural elegance and beauty of a cat, in its gentle and affectionate personality, or in its graceful body build. Another motive is a liking for unusual colors and shapes in cats.

For centuries, the cat led a relatively independent existence in both Europe and America without human interference in its procreation. As is still the case with our modern house cats, there were only a few local differences in type and color. It was not until the end of the last century that the many modern varieties of breed and color began to be developed. When there are enough animals that consistently exhibit certain characteristic traits, an international jury of cat breeders and judges recognizes them as a separate breed. To maintain the special qualities of the breed, rules are then laid down as to how a cat of that breed should look and what traits are desirable and undesirable in it. These rules are called the "standard" of the breed.

The governing bodies of the different cat associations work out the standards for each breed.

The United States has eight governing bodies, of which the CFA is by far the largest, with many affiliated cat clubs. Besides establishing the different cat standards, the CFA trains and appoints judges, authorizes shows across the country, controls a nationwide scoring system in its affiliated clubs' shows, and publishes the excellent *CFA Yearbook.*

Other important governing bodies are the American Cat Association (the oldest body in the United States), the American Cat Fanciers' Association, Inc., the Cat Fanciers' Federation, Inc., the Crown Cat Fanciers' Federation, and the United Cat Federation, Inc.

These groups cooperate closely with each other and with the Canadian Cat Association, so it is now possible for Canadian cats to enter shows in the United States and for American cats to enter shows in Canada. The CFA also cooperates closely with the FIFe, and the two organizations use each other's judges.

The following cat breeds are recognized by the CFA:

Natural breeds. Abyssinian, American Shorthair, Egyptian Mau, Japanese Bobtail, Maine Coon, Manx, Persian, Russian Blue, Turkish Angora, and Siamese.

Established breeds. Balinese, Birman, British Shorthair, Burmese, Havana Brown, Korat, and Somali.

Mutations. American Wirehair, Rex, and Scottish Fold.

House Cats and Pedigreed Cats

Hybrids. Bombay, Colorpoint Shorthair, Exotic Shorthair, Himalayan, and Oriental Shorthair.

The CFA and other governing cat bodies issue exact guidelines not only on what a cat should look like (standard), but also on how many points are to be assigned to *head* (profile, wedge, muzzle, size, ears, chin, width between the eyes), *eyes* (shape, size, slant, and placement), *body* (structure and size, including neck, muscle tone, legs and feet, tail), *coat* (length, texture) and *color* (body color, point color—matching points of dense color, proper foot pads and nose leather—and eye color) for each breed. As an example, the Point Score of the Balinese looks like this:

Point Score (CFA)

Head (20)	
Long flat profile	6
Wedge, fine muzzle, size	5
Ears	4
Chin	3
Width between eyes	2
Eyes (5)	
Shape, size, slant, and placement	5
Body (30)	
Structure and size, including neck	12
Muscle tone	10
Legs and feet	5
Tail	3
Coat (20)	
Length	10
Texture	10
Color (25)	
Body color	10
Point color—matching points of dense color, proper food pads and nose leather	10
Eye color	5
	100

Coat Colors and Patterns of House Cats and Pedigreed Cats

Unicolored Cats

Unicolored cats can be black, white, blue (blue-grey), brown, chocolate, lilac, red, or cream. Breeders call cats "blue" that in ordinary parlance would be described as being uniformly light gray. Unicolored pedigreed cats must not have any trace of another color, no stripes and no white mark on the chest; not even single white hairs are allowed.

Bicolored Cats

Cats that have some white in combination with a color are common among both house cats and pedigreed cats. The extent of the white varies. There are cats that are almost completely white with only small areas of colored fur (Turkish Van Cat, page 122), and there are dark cats with only small white markings like a blaze on the face, a white bib, or white feet.

Breeders of purebred cats try to achieve a "harmonious" distribution of colors: the white is supposed to make up about one third of the entire coat, and a lot more or a lot less white is considered undesirable. However, a white triangle on the face is always a plus. House cats with a tiger pattern often have white spots, but in pedigreed cats with officially recognized stripes or "wild" coloring, the standard does not permit white spots.

Another common combination of colors in both common and pedigreed cats is red and black (tortoiseshell) and blue and cream. Since the colors red and cream are sex-linked, animals with these colors are always female. The ideal tortoiseshell marking for a pedigreed cat is a distribution of the colors that is as even and highly contrasting as possible. In blue-cream cats, the two colors are supposed to be mingled throughout without forming definite patches of one or the other color.

Tricolored Cats

In tricolored house cats, the tortoiseshell or blue-cream coloring is combined with white patches (photograph, front cover). For genetic reasons these cats, like the tortoiseshells, are always female, and in the countryside they are responsible for a large share of the annual crop of unwanted kittens.

Tricolored mother cats are also popular with breeders of pedigreed cats because their litters are so varied. There is a combination of tabby pattern with red or reddish brown patches that is called a Tortie Tabby (photograph, page 20), but it is not yet recognized as a pedigreed breed. These animals, too, are always female.

Cats with Points

Since the Siamese coloration—light coat with dark areas on the head, tail, and paws— is a recessive trait (photographs, pages 10 and 38), this race can be maintained only through the breeding efforts of people. This pattern of coloration does not occur in house cats, but other kinds of animals have comparable markings. There are, for instance, pure white rabbits with black ears, muzzles, noses, tails, and feet, the so-called Russian or Himalayan rabbits. These animals are all born white, and the dark points develop gradually on the cooler extremities.

Cats with Markings and White Patches

Birmans (photographs, pages 37 and 128) have Siamese coloration combined with white on all four feet. But this special, regular white marking of the feet cannot be produced with consistency, and there are always some animals with white on the head or tail or with irregular white stockings or gloves.

Another breed, still considered controversial, that combines Siamese coloring with irregular white patches all over is the Ragdoll.

Cats with Tipping

Tipping means that the tips of the hairs are of a color different from the rest of the hairs. The tipping can be of any typical cat color, but black tipping is most common as in Chinchillas (photograph, page 110), Silver-Shaded, and Smoke (photograph, page 110). Cameos and Red or Cream Smoke Persians have red or cream tipping. It depends on the extent or length of the tipping whether the cat is called a Chinchilla, a Silver-Shaded, or a Smoke.

In pedigreed cats the tipping occurs in many different colors like the blue in the Blue Chinchilla.

In house cats only Black Smoke seems to occur with any frequency, and I have never yet encountered any other kind of tipping among them.

Tipping		
Length of Tipping	Color of Tipping	
	Red or cream	Black
1/8 of hair	Shell Cameo	Chinchilla
1/3 (1/8. 1/2) of hair	Shaded Cameo	Shaded Silver
more than 1/2 and up to 2/3 of hair	Red or Cream Smoke	Smoke

Striped Cats — Tabbies

A coat pattern that is very common in house cats is stripes, also called tiger or tabby markings. It goes back to the time when cats lived wild and provides excellent camouflage outside. Stripes and spots occur in wild, house, and pedigreed cats.

In this wild or "agouti" coloring there are two or three light and dark bands on each hair, with the tip always dark. This band pattern is also called ticking. There are four different groups of tabbies: mackerel, striped, or tiger tabby—the pattern of the European wild cat *(Felis silvestris)*; blotched or classic tabby; spotted tabby; and Abyssinian tabby (without markings).

The tabby pattern is very common both in house cats and pedigreed cats. Left: mackerel tabby pattern. Middle: classic or blotched tabby pattern. Right: spotted tabby pattern.

House Cats and Pedigreed Cats

Mackerel Tabby. The stripes are clearly set off. There is a straight dark line running down the back from the head to the base of the tail with several dark stripes branching off down the sides. The legs have regular stripes across them and the tail has even rings and a dark tip. On the stomach there are two rows of dark dots. The tabby also has a marking on the face that looks like an "M" and clear dark lines running to the ears. On the chest there are two bands that look like a necklace.

Blotched Tabby. With very variable stripes and patches, this cat is also called Classic Tabby. This type of marking seems to come closest to the most common wild markings. The big difference between this pattern and the tiger tabby is that there are unmistakeable dark patches on the shoulders and sides. These patches are rimmed by one or several lines. The markings on the head, legs, tail, and stomach are the same as on the Mackerel Tabby. This pattern is usually found in Oriental and European type short-haired breeds.

Spotted Tabby. This kind of tabby (photograph, page 10) has lots of dark dots, round or oval, that are clearly set off from each other all over the body and legs. In the case of pedigreed cats, the more dots the better. The shape of the dots should be uniform. The legs are striped, and the forehead bears an "M," and a narrow, dark line runs down the back.

Abyssinian Tabby. It is almost devoid of dark pattern or markings on the body (photograph, page 91). All hairs are banded with the exception of the underbelly, where the hairs are light and unicolored. The Abyssinian has dark patches, stripes, or markings of any kind only on the forelegs, low on the flanks, and on the tail.

The Somali has the same coat pattern as the Abyssinian Tabby (photograph, page 127).

For the colors and markings of various breeds, see the Table on pages 134–135.

Long-haired Cats

Persians, Some Recognized Colors

All Persians, no matter what color, have the same build. The head is round and large, with a broad skull and a round face. The neck is short and thick. The small, round ears that point forward are not too broad at the base and sit low on the head; they have long tufts of hair which, however, grow not from the tips as in the lynx but from the base of the ear. Large, round, and wide-open eyes lend the face a childlike expression. The nose is short, flat, and broad. Typical for the profile of a Persian is the break between forehead and nose, called the "stop." Full cheeks, a strong and well-developed chin, and wide, powerful jaws are also typical for the head of a Persian. There should be no abnormalities in the teeth and jaws.

The body is medium large to large. However, what counts is not size but harmoniousness of overall appearance. The body is powerful and supported by short, sturdy, and straight legs. The shoulders and the rest of the body are evenly proportioned with a well-rounded middle and a straight back. The paws are large and round. The front paws have five toes; the rear paws, four. The toes are set closely together and have long tufts between them. The tail is bushy and short, without bends, kinks, or knots.

Point Score for Maine Coon Cats (CFA)

Head (including size and shape of eyes, ear shape and set)	30
Type (including shape, size, bone and length of tail)	20
Coat	10
Balance	5
Refinement	5
Color	20
Eye color	10

In all tabby varieties, the 20 points for color are to be divided 10 for markings and 10 for color (CFA).

House Cats and Pedigreed Cats

The fur of a Persian is long, thick, and fine. It stands out from the body and has a silky sheen. The hair is about the same length all over the body, forming a particularly impressive neck ruff.

Of the thirty-six recognized color variations of Persians, some of the most important are:

Black Persian. This is one of the first long-haired breeds to be developed in Europe. Black Persians look particularly stunning if their coat is a deep black and their eyes are a bright coppery brown. This beautiful contrast is hardly ever present in young cats and develops only with age. Young cats often look brownish or gray, and the color of their eyes is not yet a pure, brilliant copper. Black Persians that spend a lot of time in the sunlight also appear brownish or develop so-called "ghost markings," a faint tabby pattern in the black fur that is undesirable.

Black Persians must not be powdered before an exhibition because this gives the black a gray look. Instead they should be bathed two or three days before being shown.

White Persian. White Persians are direct descendants of the Angoras of Asia Minor that were highly popular with the ladies of the Constantinople harems. The first White Persians to be imported to Europe were of the original type with blue eyes (photograph, page 109). White Persians with copper eyes have been recognized as a separate variety since 1938. This eye color was obtained by crossing blue-eyed White Persians with Black or Blue Persians. White Persians with different colored eyes – a phenomenon that is limited to white cats – have one blue and one copper eye with equal color depth. These "odd-eyed" animals are the result of crossing a blue-eyed with a copper-eyed Persian or of pairing a Blue Persian with a white, blue-eyed cat. Blue-eyed White Persians are often congenitally deaf, a defect that breeders try to eliminate by introducing copper-eyed Persians into the strain.

The care of White Persians is just the same as that of any other long-haired cats. However, the tail, particularly of male cats, has to be powdered often because these cats tend to develop stud tail (page 25), which causes the tail to look yellowish. A White Persian should be powdered carefully before being exhibited. Many breeders claim that baths are necessary, but I know a stud that became an International Champion without ever having had a bath. White Persians are relaxed and sensitive cats and no more delicate than other Persians. Still, they are better kept in an apartment.

Blue Persian. Blue Persians (photograph, page 110) are one of today's most popular long-haired cats, and at shows they are usually very well represented. According to Pietro della Valle, the first importer of Blue Persians, these cats lived in various Persian provinces as early as the sixteenth century. But the Blue Persian type of today dates back only to the end of the last century. The English first recognized the breed at the Crystal Palace show of 1888 in London. Breeding has been supervised very carefully since then with the result that Blue Persians are now considered the best type of Persian and are frequently used to improve the type of other colors. It is difficult to obtain an evenly colored blue coat; usually it contains some difference of shading, which is considered a flaw. The overall shade of blue (lighter or darker) is unimportant, however. The eye color, as in all but White Persians with both eyes of the same color, is brilliant copper. Since the Persian traits are sometimes overdeveloped in these cats—a nose that is too short and an overly pronounced stop—the eyes tend to tear. Blue Persians are known for their easy tempers and their intelligence. They like to be part of the family and are happiest when they are the center of attention.

Many breeders bathe their animals before exhibitions; others merely apply talcum or baby powder and then brush it out carefully.

Red Persian. Red Persians (photograph, page 110) were already known in England around 1880, in the early days of pedigreed cats, but they were called Orange Persians then. The most difficult part of breeding Reds is to achieve a dark, uniform red without any tabby pattern (page 114). The eye color is brilliant copper. Around 1933, the well-known German breeder Konrad Hirschmann regularly showed beautiful specimens of this breed, but during the Second World War his stock was destroyed.

House Cats and Pedigreed Cats

The breed was neglected for about twenty years but has come into its own again, and one now often sees Reds free of markings at exhibitions. Young cats up to eighteen months old often have undesirable tabby markings. Red cats are also interesting genetically because their color is sex-linked (page 101).

Preparing Red Persians for showing is difficult. Some authorities recommend rubbing warm bran into the fur, brushing it out again, and polishing the coat with a chamois cloth, always stroking with the lie of the fur, never against it.

Cream Persian. The original color of the Cream Persian, when the cat was first noted, around 1900, was fawn. Today's cream color was achieved through long selective breeding in England. The modern Cream Persian, with its uniformly buff cream coloring, brilliant copper eyes, and excellent type, counts among the most popular breeds. Unfortunately, one often sees Cream Persians that are too "hot," meaning they are too dark. The color cream, like red, is a sex-linked trait since it is a "dilution" of red (page 101).

Black Smoke Persian. The Black Smoke Persian (photograph, page 110) is one of the oldest pedigreed cats. It was first described as early as 1860, and the first Smoke Champion dates back to 1890. This cat, which is sometimes called the cat of contrasts, has a black face with brilliant copper eyes. The face is surrounded by a silver ruff. The coat appears black, but when the cat moves, the white undercoat shows through. The Smoke is one of the "tipped" breeds (page 114), as are the Chinchilla and the Cameo. I have often seen Smoke Persians carry off the "Best in Show" title because their beauty is impressive indeed. While young, Smokes often have poorly colored coats that are too light and have spots or stripes. They develop their full beauty only gradually.

For preparations for showing, see page 23. At present, ten different color varieties are recognized in Europe, and four (Black, Blue, Red, and Tortoiseshell Smoke) in the United States.

Cameo Persian. Cameos first appeared in the United States around 1934, have been systematically bred from 1950 on, and have been recognized in the United States since 1960. Cameos are a color variation of black-tipped Persians with the tips of the hairs being red or cream instead of black.

If the undercoat is white and sufficiently tipped with red on back, flanks, head, and tail to give the cat a sparkling appearance, we are dealing with a Shell Cameo, also called a Red Chinchilla. Its face and legs may be very slightly shaded with tipping. Chin, ear tufts, stomach, and chest are white.

The undercoat of the Shaded Cameo or Red Shaded, however, is white with a mantle of red tipping shading down the sides, face, and tail from dark on the ridge to white on the chin, chest, stomach, and under the tail. The legs should be of the same tone as the face. The general effect must be redder than the Shell Cameo.

Silver Tabby Persian. Although Silver Tabby Persians are one of the oldest breeds, they are now seen only rarely at shows. Getting a clearly tabby marking (page 114) on a silver ground together with the desired Persian traits is difficult. It also takes a lot of know-how to obtain the desired green eye color. Silver Tabbies are relatively undemanding, and the births are usually unproblematical. The newborn kittens are black and have stripes only on the sides and legs. The tabby pattern does not emerge until the kittens are four to six months old, and kittens with clear markings often turn out to have poor markings when grown.

Silver Tabbies should be brushed with the lie of the fur before being exhibited to accentuate the tabby markings.

Brown Tabby Persian. At the end of the last century, Brown Tabbies were very popular, but they no doubt looked very different from the cats that go by this name today. They looked much more like ordinary house cats with long fur. The black markings on sand-colored ground typical of these cats forms a lovely contrast. Brown Tabbies are known for being extremely robust and healthy and for their intelligence and their affectionate natures. Consequently, this tabby is getting more and more popular and is found in increasing numbers at exhibitions. As with all tabbies, it is difficult to achieve both clear markings and excellent Persian traits, and there are few tabbies with perfect Persian heads and dark orange eyes.

Like all other tabbies, this one, too, should be brushed with the lie of the fur before exhibitions. This brings out the tabby pattern best.

Blue Tabby Persian. In Europe, the Blue Tabby has been officially recognized only since 1980, and it is therefore one of the newest Persian varieties. In America it has been recognized since 1962. The tabby markings in this cat are so clear that it is never taken for a Blue Persian, a confusion that arises often between Red Tabbies and Reds. The markings of a Blue Tabby are not blue on blue but blue on ivory, providing the vivid contrast that an excellent representative of this variety is expected to display. The eyes should be dark orange to brilliant copper-colored.

This cat, too, is brushed with the lie of the fur before exhibitions so that the fur almost hugs the body and shows the markings to good advantage.

Golden Persian. Coat color: undercoat, a warm cream; fur on back, sides, head and tail with such strong, dark brown tipping (page 114) that the cat looks golden. A distinction is made between Shell Golden and Shaded Golden. The legs have some weak shadings; the chin, ear tufts, chest, and belly are cream-colored, and the eyes, lips, and nose have dark brown rims. The nose leather is a dark rose, and the pads on the feet are dark brown. The eyes are green or blue-green. The Golden Persian is one of the most recent varieties of Persians.

Red Tabby Persian. In the early days of breeding pedigreed cats, plain Red and Red Tabby Persians were considered one breed. But there is a clear difference between the two varieties—namely the tabby markings (page 114)—although it is not genetically fixed. In contrast to tabbies of other colors, the tabby pattern of Red Tabbies is not a true marking but a kind of ''ghost marking'' that is often found in unicolored kittens and is undesirable in them. It sometimes happens that a cat changes back several times in the course of its life between Red and Red Tabby, and often neither the judge nor the breeder can decide for sure whether a particular cat is a Red Persian with undesirable stripes

or a Red Tabby with markings that are too faint. It is therefore a matter of sheer luck whether or not two Red Tabby parents will produce Red Tabby kittens or not. The eyes are dark orange to copper-colored.

Red Tabbies should not be powdered—this dulls their sheen—or brushed against the lie of the fur, which would obscure the outlines of the markings. A smooth, shiny coat brings out the tabby pattern best.

Chinchilla Persian. The Chinchilla (photograph, page 110) is one of the most attractive Persians. It is basically a white cat, but the tip of each hair is black (page 114). Chinchillas are somewhat more temperamental but no more delicate than other color varieties. They were first bred from Smoke Persians at the end of the last century but were considerably darker at that time and had striped legs. Kittens are born with tiger markings, but these disappear later on. The cats have to be at least five to seven months old before their Chinchilla coloration is fully developed. One unusual trait of these Persians is that they have green or blue-green eyes with black rims around them, as well as a black rim around the brick red nose leather.

A Chinchilla has to be meticulously groomed before exhibitions. It should be bathed one week ahead of time and then powdered down to the skin with talcum or baby powder every day. Brush out the powder carefully. On the eve of the exhibition, the cat gets one last vigorous brushing to remove the last traces of powder.

Shaded Silver Persian. Shaded Silver Persians turned up at exhibitions as early as the turn of the century. In those early days there was hardly any difference between Chinchillas and Shaded Silver Persians. If you imagine a very dark Chinchilla, you have the very picture of a Shaded Silver, the difference being the length of the tipping (page 114). A Shaded Silver cannot have any stripes, patches, or streaks, and the dark tips of the hairs have to be evenly distributed. Kittens are born with pronounced tabby markings all over, but these disappear later just as they do in Chinchillas. The undercoat is pure white and is covered with black tipping. Ringlets that do not go all around the legs are permitted. The face and the upper side of the

House Cats and Pedigreed Cats

tail must be tipped, and the chin, chest, belly, inside of the legs, and underside of the tail must be pure white.

Preparations for exhibitions are the same as for Chinchillas.

Tortoiseshell Persian. The mating of red and black cats produces Tortoiseshells, which—for genetic reasons—are always female (page 101). The only thing I know about the history of Tortoiseshell Persians is that this breed first appeared around 1900. At that time they were used only for breeding Red and Cream Persians. It was some time before their own special beauty was recognized and they were bred systematically. Today Tortoiseshells, or Torties, are one of the most popular breeds and are represented in large numbers at cat shows. They are popular not only with breeders but also with all kinds of pet owners who enjoy these colorful cats with their copper-colored eyes.

All that is needed for this cat's grooming is a brush with natural bristles and a comb. Powder should not be used. If powdering does become necessary, use a special powder (page 24).

Tortoiseshell Persians also come in Chocolate and Lilac.

Tortoiseshell and White Persian. In olden days, this colorful cat was supposed to bring good luck and the superstition holds even today in Japan. No wonder, then, that this long-haired variety became a candidate for systematic breeding. In the United States it was recognized relatively late (in 1956), and the color combination was long considered a flaw. The colors red, cream, and black are supposed to be evenly interspersed with white, and a white patch on the back is desirable. No more than two thirds of the coat should be colored, and no more than half may be white. A white blaze on the face is a plus, and the eyes should be dark orange. Grooming for exhibition should be done basically as described on page 24, and powder should be used sparingly or not at all because it blurs the contrast between the white and the colors.

In addition to tortoiseshell and white there are also the color combinations blue, tortoiseshell, and white; chocolate, tortoiseshell, and white; and lilac, tortoiseshell, and white.

Blue Tortoiseshell and White Persian. This variety derives from the same strain as the Tortoiseshell and White (above). Here, the colors red and black have been "diluted" (which means lightened, page 99) into cream and blue. This variety is sometimes also called Tricolor because the three colors blue, cream, and white are distributed in patches all over the body. This popular variety is seen in increasing numbers at cat shows.

Preparations for exhibition are the same as described under Tortoiseshell and White (above).

Bicolor Persian. Bicolors (photograph, page 110) were shown at the very earliest cat shows, but they had no name of their own then. They were displayed as "Persians, Other Colors," and when they were first systematically bred, the ideal coloring breeders aimed for was something that resembled Dutch Rabbits as much as possible. But for genetic reasons—Dutch piebald markings occur only in rabbits—this goal was impossible to reach. Bicolor Persians were first given standards of their own in England in 1971. Today this breed is one of the most popular Persians. Bicolors are usually healthy, long-lived cats that give their owners much pleasure. There are six colors—black, blue, chocolate, lilac, red, and cream—all with white.

Powder should not be used on them in preparation for showing. It blurs the contrast between the white and the color. Otherwise grooming is the same as for other Persians (page 23).

Blue Cream Persian. The Blue Cream has been around since about 1920, and it was recognized in England as a pedigreed cat around 1930. Blue Creams also are always females because of the sex-linked color (page 000). By European standards, the colors are supposed to be intermingled in the Blue Cream to give the impression of one overall mixture. Cream patches on the face or the paws are frowned upon. The eyes are deep copper or orange as in the Tortoiseshell. In America the desired color arrangement is different: blue with solid cream patches, clearly defined and well-broken. The Persian type traits are usually well-developed in Blue Creams, and kittens especially display the desired childlike facial expression.

The coat of a Blue Cream is powdered before an

exhibition to make it fluffy and light, and the powder is carefully brushed out so that the silky sheen is maintained.

Chocolate Persian. These cats were obtained by mating Persians with Havanna cats (page 133), a slender short-haired type that contributed to the new Persian variety not only its brown color but also its elegant, slender build. Developing an excellent Persian type from this crossing represented a challenging and arduous task, and it was equally difficult to retain the desired copper eye color. The Dutch and the English began breeding these Chocolate Longhairs some years ago, and these interesting cats are shown more and more frequently at exhibitions.

Lilac Persian. The coat of this variety is a light lavender with a pink cast; the eyes are brilliant copper. Chocolates and Lilacs are often raised by the same breeders because these two colors are closely related genetically. In both varieties the type is improved when individuals with the best color and type are mated.

Persians, Nonrecognized Colors (European)

Cats whose colors do not belong in any recognized variety, and that therefore have no standard, are placed in the category "Persians, other colors." These cats are usually the results of accidental matings or of breeding experiments. Any cat with a new color is first placed in this group, and, when it is exhibited, it is judged in a separate class. What counts in the judging is the type: the cat has to look like a true Persian (page 115). It is impossible to describe all the nonrecognized color varieties; and I should like to mention only those that are most popular in Europe, many of which are already recognized as official breeds in the United States:

Calico Persian. Coat white, with clearly defined black and red patches; white predominates on the underside; eyes, a bright copper. Recognized in the United States.

Diluted Calico Persian (Blue-cream and white). Coat white, with clearly defined blue and cream patches; white predominates on the underside; eyes, a bright copper. Recognized in the United States.

Van Bicolor Persian (Harlequin). Coat black and white, red and white, blue and white, or cream and white, with the white restricted to the head, tail, and legs; one or two small spots on the body are permitted. Recognized in the United States.

Van Calico Persian. Coat white, with uniform black and red spots only on the head, legs, and tail; one or two small spots on the body are permitted.

Van Blue Persian (Cream and White). Coat white, with clearly defined blue and cream spots on the head, tail, and legs only; one or two small spots on the body are permitted. Recognized in the United States.

Peke Face Persian, Red, and Red Tabby. Although this type of cat is included among the Persians in the United States, its head is not described as being typically Persian; instead it is supposed to look as much as possible like that of a Pekinese dog (hence the name). The color and markings are those of a Red or Red Tabby Persian (pages 116, 118). The nose should be very short and depressed, or indented between the eyes, and the muzzle noticeably wrinkled. The eyes are large and round, orange in color, widely spaced, prominent and brilliant. Recognized in the United States.

Cameo Tabby Persian. Coat ground color off-white, with red tabby markings. Nose and pads, rose; eyes, brilliant copper. Recognized in the United States.

Himalayans

Himalayan/Colorpoint Longhair. The Himalayan/Colorpoint Longhair (photograph, page 110) is one of the most recent creations of English breeders, and the popularity of this breed, which was recognized in the country of its origin in 1955, keeps growing. Since the Siamese (page 132) is perhaps the favorite short-haired breed, the idea

House Cats and Pedigreed Cats

of crossing it with a Persian was an obvious one, and it is this crossing that produced the Himalayan/Colorpoint Longhair. It was quite difficult and took a lot of patience to derive a true Persian type from the slender Siamese, but finally breeders succeeded in creating cats that look like Persians but have the coat and eye coloring of Siamese cats. Still, Colorpoints with rather pointed heads do turn up now and then. These cats, of course, fall short of the standards for their breed. Colorpoints are bred in many different shades. Because they are devoted to people and are friendly and sociable, these cats are very popular pets.

Grooming is very simple. Regular brushing and an occasional powdering maintain this cat's charming good looks.

Point Score for All Himalayans (CFA)

Head (including size and shape of eyes, ears, ear shape and set)	30
Type (including shape, size, bone, and length of tail)	20
Coat	10
Body color	10
Point color	10
Eye color	10
Balance	5
Refinement	5

Medium Long-haired Cats

These cats, though long-haired, do not belong with the Persians and Himalayans, as the absence of the flat face typical of Persians reveals at first glance. Members of this group are the Birman, the Turkish Van Cat, the Norwegian Forest Cat, the Somali, the Maine Coon, and the Balinese.

Birman. This cat (photograph, pages 37, 128) is sometimes called the "holy" Birman, and there is a charming legend about its origin:

Long before the birth of Buddha, an old Kattah priest lived in the mountains of Indo-

china with his white cat Sinh. The priest often meditated together with Sinh before the statue of Tsun-Kyan-Kse, the goddess of reincarnation. One day, while lost in deep prayer, the priest was murdered by a band of robbers. Sinh immediately leaped from its fallen master to the throne of Tsun-Kyan-Kse, and as it did so the miracle of transmigration took place. The white fur of the cat turned golden like the goddess, and its eyes took on the sapphire blue of the goddess's eyes. Legs, tail, nose, and ears turned the color of the earth. The tips of the feet, with which the cat had touched the white head of its master, were the only part to stay white. On that same day all the holy temple cats took on the appearance of the faithful Sinh.

Touching as this legend may be, the origin of the Birman cat appears to be more prosaic. This cat is said to have been bred in France from Siamese and Persians. Birmans supposedly go back to 1919, and they have been systematically bred in France since 1930. They first showed up in England in 1960. Nadine de Khlaramour was the first Birman to come to Germany. She arrived there in 1963 and became the ancestress of many Birmans all over the world. I have seen grandchildren and great-grandchildren of hers even as far away as Australia.

The coat markings of the Birman are very similar to those of the Colorpoint (page 120), but its head is not as broad, and the nose is longer. A Birman is supposed to resemble neither the Siamese nor the Persians in type, and should have a long but stocky body. The most obvious feature distinguishing it from all other breeds is that it wears white gloves on all four feet. These gloves should be of equal height, and the ones on the hind feet should extend up the hock in pointed spurs. The eyes are a deep blue, a sign of partial albinism. Birmans come in the colors Seal point, Blue point, Chocolate point, and Lilac point. The fur is long but not quite as long as that of Persians, and it does not have the Persian tendency to mat. Birmans can therefore be let outdoors without any problems. People sometimes refer to it jokingly as an "easy care" cat because it does not have to be combed. Some brushing is all it takes to keep the coat nice and silky.

Birmans are more spirited than Persians, and

121

House Cats and Pedigreed Cats

they get along easily with other pets. My little Birman tomcat spends summers together with my two house cats on a farm and has developed a great attachment to our Haflinger pony mare. He likes to sit underneath her without the slightest sign of fear of what her shod feet might do.

Point Score for Birmans (CFA)

Head (including size and shape of eyes, ear shape, and set)	30
Type (including shape, size, bone, and length of tail)	25
Coat	10
Color	25
Eye color	10

Turkish Van Cat. This cat (photograph, page 128) comes from the Van Lake area in eastern Turkey and is therefore sometimes called simply the "Van Cat." English visitors who liked the looks of this cat brought it to England in 1955. In Turkey this cat is not systematically bred but is simply a traditional house cat. The Turkish Cat was officially recognized in England in 1969. In the United States, however, the breed is not recognized. The first cats of this variety to be introduced into Germany came from Holland, England, and Switzerland in the late 1970s.

Because of the inhospitable landscape and the long, cold winters and hot, dry summers of its place of origin, the Turkish Cat matures very early. The five or six kittens of a typical litter are born with full adult coloring. They open their eyes as early as the fifth day after birth and will use a litter box at three weeks. By the time they are five or six weeks old, they eat chunks of meat. Their appetite is impressive, and the race is exceptionally large — cats ten months old weigh close to 10 pounds (4 kilograms).

Though affectionate and playful, Turkish Cats are known for their tempers. They do not like to be carried around, and they rebel when they are forced to do anything. Their uncat-like enjoyment of water

has earned them the designation "swimming cats." They seem to be magically drawn to moving water, and they also like to race around in the snow. If this cat is restricted to the indoors, it should be given plenty of space for romping. Ideally it should live in temperatures of 57 to 65°F (14 to 18°C) and be given a large outdoor area to roam around in and practice its excellent hunting skills. Turkish Cats are bicolored (page 113) — white with orange to auburn spots on the face and a red tail — and have amber-colored eyes.

All that is needed in the line of grooming is some brushing and an occasional powdering.

Norwegian Forest Cat. When hiking in the mountain forests of Norway not far from the Arctic Circle, we often met Norwegian Forest Cats (photograph, inside back cover) in the vicinity of isolated farms. These cats live in the woods, mate with house cats, and live in the proximity of people. It seems conceivable that this cat — like the Maine Coon Cat (page 123) which it resembles — is the result of natural selection in a climate of long, hard winters. Sometimes exceptionally handsome animals are caught and used for breeding purposes. At Norwegian cat shows I have had the pleasure of judging some of these stunningly beautiful cats.

The Norwegian Forest Cat has a strong, supple, and long body, a triangular head, and a straight profile. The wooly undercoat is covered with shiny, water-repellent hair that hangs down from the back over the sides. It also has a neck ruff of longer hair, a "shirt front," a triangular beard extending down from the cheeks, and lynx-like tufts of hair on the ears. The tail is of medium length and bushy. All colors are accepted, as is white on the feet, chest, and belly. The eyes should match the coat in coloring. The thick fur has to be combed and brushed, but powdering is not appropriate.

Somali. The Somali (photograph, page 127) is a quite recent breed. It was given championship status by the CFA in October, 1928. Its fur is half long, very soft to the touch, and the coloration is the same as that of the Abyssinian. The eyes are either amber or green (page 129), almond-shaped,

House Cats and Pedigreed Cats

large and brilliant. One could describe this breed as an Abyssinian in long dress. The special feature of both these breeds is that the hairs are banded (page 115). There are two different colors of Somalis: ruddy (orange-brown tipped with black) and red (red tipped with brown).

Grooming is the same as for long-haired cats (page 23).

The Somali is a well-proportioned medium to large cat, with an alert, lively interest in its surroundings. It has an even disposition and is easy to handle.

Point Score for Somalis (CFA)

Head (25)	
Skull	6
Muzzle	6
Ears	7
Eye shape	6
Body (25)	
Torso	10
Legs and feet	10
Tail	5
Coat (25)	
Texture	10
Length	15
Color (25)	
Color	10
Ticking	10
Eye color	5

Maine Coon Cat. In spite of its name, this cat from Maine is obviously not related to coons. It is a solid and muscular cat, and its great resemblance to the Norwegian Forest Cat suggests that the two races are descended from common ancestors. Sailors may have brought European long-haired cats — either Norwegian Forest Cats or Turkish Angoras — to America, where these cats then interbred with indigenous ones and developed their thick fur in adaptation to the local climate. The Maine Coon is one of the oldest American breeds. It was exhibited at agricultural fairs as early as 1860, long before there were cat exhibitions. Then it was forgotten as a breed, and interest in it did not revive until the 1950s. Now the Maine Coon is getting

more and more popular, and lovely examples of this breed often turn up at exhibitions. All colors of its heavy, shaggy coat are possible, and the eyes are supposed to match the color of the individual cat.

Frequent brushing and combing of the thick fur, which should be shorter on the shoulders, longer on the stomach and britches, is the only grooming required.

Point Score for Maine Coon Cats (CFA)

Head (30)	
Shape	15
Ears	10
Eyes	5
Body (35)	
Shape	20
Neck	5
Legs and feet	5
Tail	5
Coat (20)	20
Color (15)	
Body color	10
Eye color	5

Balinese. It is said that around 1950 a fluffy mutation in a strain of purebred Siamese appeared in the United States. At first, these mutants were going to be culled, but then some owners decided to breed them systematically. They were initially called "long-haired Siamese," but later (in 1963) they were recognized in the United States under the name of Balinese. The ideal Balinese is a slim, delicate cat but lithe and muscular with elegant lines. The fur is long, fine, and silky, and there is no downy undercoat. A Balinese is essentially a Siamese with long hair. Indeed, the coloration, markings (page 114), and blue eyes are the same as in the Siamese from which the Balinese differs only in the quality of fur.

The fine, silky fur should be groomed like that of a Persian (page 23).

(See Point Score, page 113)

Turkish Angora or **Ankara Cat.** This cat, which has long been popular in Turkey, was not brought to America until the late 1960s, where it has been

House Cats and Pedigreed Cats

systematically bred since then. The Turkish Angora looks like the Persians of the old days, having a pointed head, long legs, and a long, narrow body. It has long hair, is of medium heavy build, and has a small- to medium-sized, wedge-shaped head that is broad at the top and runs to a point at the chin. A solid, firm cat, it gives the impression of grace and flowing movement. All kinds of color are possible, with eyes of matching color.

Point Score for Turkish Angoras (CFA)	
Head	35
Body	30
Color	20
Coat	15

Non-recognized Medium Long-haired Cats

Apart from the ones recognized in some countries, there are a few medium long-haired breeds that have not been officially recognized anywhere. I should like to mention the most important of these breeds.

Cymric. This cat was bred from the Manx. The Manx is a short-haired cat that lacks a tail because of an inhibitor mutation (the formation of the tail is inhibited). In addition, these cats are characterized by a "lethal factor" (page 102) in their genetic make-up; and, because of the abnormal pelvic structure that goes along with the lack of a tail, Manx cats cannot walk normally. The standard for Manx as well as Cymric cats in fact calls for a "rabbit-like or hopping gait." In Japan, tailless cats were long preferred because house cats with tails were considered too "European" (see Japanese Bobtail, page 126). I find it hard to understand why people would want to deliberately introduce the genetic defect of "taillessness" into long-haired cats, and the Cymric is in fact not recognized generally either in Europe or in the United States. There are only a few American cat clubs that have drawn up descriptions of this breed.

Ragdoll. The Ragdoll is best described as a mixture of Birman, Colorpoint, and Bicolor (pages 120 and 121). In Europe this cat would be considered an off-color and could not be used for breeding, and the CFA (page 113) does not recognize this breed either. The only standards for it were drawn up by the American "Ragdoll Cat Association." The Ragdoll is quite a new breed and probably originated from the crossing of the Persian Bicolor and Colorpoint. The coat of this breed is long or semi-long and rather heavy. The calico pattern, particularly on the legs, can be achieved only by introducing house cats or Birmans into the strain.

Short-haired Cats

There are a number of short-haired breeds, some of which bear practically no resemblance to each other except for the characteristic they all have in common, namely short hair (for grooming, see page 22). The most important short-haired breeds are: British, American, and European Shorthairs, Russian Blue, Abyssinian, Manx, Rex, and Korat. In addition there are the Oriental Shorthairs and the Siamese, both of which differ from all the above-mentioned cats by having a slender, delicate, and extremely elegant shape. These two breeds are discussed in separate sections (pages 132, 133).

Recognized Short-haired Breeds

British Shorthair. Short-haired cats have been deliberately bred for a long time in Europe. The most popular colors were bred before the turn of the century. Since the English, who were the pioneers of cat breeding, favored a plump, sturdy type, the British cats developed in this direction and were called British Shorthair (photograph, page 127). Initially British breeders produced primarily blue-gray cats, and in Germany these blue British cats are generally known as "Kartäuser." They are not identical with the Chartreuse. The different colors were achieved by mating house cats with Persians that were particularly stout and round-headed. Since these hybrids have recessive genes for long hair, it is not surprising that even today matings of British Shorthairs sometimes produce long-haired kittens. In breeding these cats it is particularly important to try to keep the strain for shorthairedness pure.

The British Shorthair has a large body with a muscular, wide chest; the shoulders and back are stout, the legs and feet sturdy, and the paws round and strong. The tail is short and thick and rounded at the tip. The broad, round head sits on a short neck. The nose is broad and has a slight dip but no stop. The ears are round and wide and are rounded at the tips. All British Shorthairs have dark orange eyes except for the Silver Tabby, the British Tipped ("Shorthair Chinchilla"), and the British Tipped Shaded, all of which have green or yellowish green eyes. White British Shorthairs, like White Persians, are bred to have orange or blue eyes or to be odd-eyed (one orange and one blue eye). The thick, fine fur with its thick undercoat stands off from the body like the pile of plush. British Shorthairs are bred in almost all colors.

Point Score for British Shorthairs (CFA)

Head (30)	
Muzzle	5
Skull	5
Ears	5
Neck	5
Eye shape	10
Body (30)	
Torso	20
Legs and feet	5
Tail	5
Coat (20)	
Length	10
Texture	10
Color (20)	20

American Shorthair. Immigrants from Europe took their cats along to North America, where these animals, just like the European house cats, developed without human interference. Only much later did people take a new interest in cats and breed them seriously for certain traits. The American Shorthair is not recognized in Europe although it is quite similar to the European Shorthair.

It is believed by some naturalists to be the original breed of domestic cat. It has for many, many centuries adapted itself willingly and cheerfully to the needs of man, but without allowing itself to become effete or its natural intelligence to diminish. Its disposition and habits are exemplary as a house pet, a pet and companion for children, but the feral instinct lies not too far beneath the surface and this breed of cat remains capable of self-sufficiency when the need arises. Its hunting instinct is so strong that it exercises the skill even when well provided with food. This is our only breed of true "working cat."

The conformation of the breed is well adapted for this and reflects its refusal to surrender its natural functions. This is a cat lithe enough to stalk its prey, but powerful enough to make the kill easily. Its reflexes are under perfect control. Its legs are long enough to cope with any terrain and heavy and muscular enough for high leaps. The face is long enough to permit easy grasping by the teeth with jaws so powerful they can close against resistance. Its coat is dense enough to protect from moisture, cold and superficial skin injuries, but short enough and of sufficiently hard texture to resist matting or entanglement when slipping through heavy vegetation. No part of the anatomy is so exaggerated as to foster weakness. The general effect is that of the trained athlete, with all muscles rippling easily beneath the skin, the flesh lean and hard, and with great latent power held in reserve.

Point Score for American Shorthairs (CFA)

Head (including size and shape of eyes, ear shape, and set and structure of nose)	30
Type (including shape, size, bone and length of tail)	25
Coat	15
Color	20
Eye color	10

American Wirehair. One day in the mid-1970s, a genetic mutation turned up in a litter of ordinary American house cats: the fur of these kittens had the consistency of that of a wire-haired terrier or

House Cats and Pedigreed Cats

wire-haired dachshund, a trait that had never before been observed in cats. The coat is springy, dense, resilient, and coarse. The wiry hair was due to a mutation of genes comparable to that which produces curly hair in Rex cats. These wire-haired cats were then bred deliberately in America, and a standard drawn up by a Wirehair club.

Point Score for American Wirehairs (CFA)

Head (including size and shape of eyes, ear shape and set)	25
Type (including shape, size, bone and length of tail)	20
Coat	45
Color and eye color	10

Bombay. The Bombay was created by crossing Burmese with American Shorthairs. This cat occurs only in black, and the most important criterion in judging Bombay cats is the color and quality of their fur, which should be very close-lying with a shimmering patent leather sheen no other black cat possesses.

Point Score for Bombays (CFA)

Head and ears (25)	
Round of head	9
Full face and proper profile	9
Ears	7
Eyes (5)	
Placement and shape	5
Body (15)	
Body	10
Tail	5
Coat (20)	
Shortness	10
Texture	5
Close-lying	5
Color (35)	
Body color	20
Eye color	15

Egyptian Mau. The Egyptian Mau is a spotted cat (page 114) that was developed from house cats. This is the only thing we can say with certainty about this cat's ancestry. Some people claim that this strain was the result of systematic breeding of cats that had been imported from Egypt, while others say that the crossing of Tabbypoint Siamese (page 10) with house cats or Burmese (page 130) produced the Egyptian Mau. Egyptian reliefs often include a spotted cat that stands for the sun god Ra, and the goal of modern breeders is to revive a breed that existed in Egypt around 2000 B.C.

Point Score for Egyptian Maus

Head (20)	
Muzzle	5
Skull	5
Ears	5
Eye shape	5
Body (25)	
Torso	10
Legs and feet	10
Tail	5
Coat (10)	
Texture and length	10
Pattern (25)	25
Color (20)	
Eye color	5
Coat color	15

Japanese Bobtail. For many centuries, there have been bobtailed cats in Japan, where they are said to bring good luck, although these cats originally came from China. In 1969, they were introduced into the United States, where they are now bred. The unique set of its eyes, combined with high cheekbones, lends a distinctive Japanese cast to its face, especially in profile. The special feature of this breed is its thick stump of a tail that looks a little like a powder puff. Bobtails occur in different colors; the most popular in Japan is a tricolored cat that is white with orange and black patches. Bicolored Bobtails also have a long tradition in Japan (photograph, page 127).

Short-haired and medium-haired cats. ▷
Above left: Cornish Rex, red and white. Above right: Japanese Bobtail. Middle left: British Shorthair, blue-cream. Middle right: British Shorthair. Below left: British Shorthair, red tabby. Below right: two Somali cats.

126

Point Score for Japanese Bobtails (CFA)

Head	20
Type	30
Tail	20
Color and markings	20
Coat	10

Scottish Fold. This cat with folded ears is a relatively recent mutation that originated in Scotland around 1960. It is easy to spot by the unusual characteristic that gives it its name: ears that are folded forward and lend these cats an amusing expression. This mutation is dominant (page 98), and Scottish Folds are bred seriously in the United States.

Point Score for Scottish Folds (CFA)

Ears	30
Head	20
Eyes	15
Body and tail	25
Color	10

Russian Blue. Although the Russian Blue is built much less powerfully and has green eyes, it is sometimes taken for a Chartreuse. The remarkable feature of this cat is its coat, which is short, thick, very fine and soft, shines like silk, and stands off the body like the pile of plush. The nose leather and the pads on the feet are bluish gray as in all blue cats. All that is known about the origin of this cat is that it does not come from Russia. This breed is widely kept in the United States, England, and Northern Europe.

Point Score for Russian Blues (CFA)

Head and neck	20
Body type	20
Eye shape	5
Ears	5
Coat	20
Color	20
Eye color	10

Abyssinian. With a coloring very similar to that of wild animals and therefore often called "rabbit cat," the Abyssinian (photograph, page 91) is today one of the most popular cats. Its fur does indeed resemble that of wild rabbits. We suspect that the Abyssinian was deliberately bred by humans although it looks very much like the cats depicted by the Egyptians in their murals. In our day there are no cats living wild in Ethiopia (Abyssinia) that resemble the Abyssinian cat, and that is why I assume that this breed is the result of selective breeding in Europe. Abyssinians were first described in England in 1874, and they have been intensively bred there since 1926. But Abyssinians are relatively rare even today because their litters are small. Their uncomplicated, affectionate nature makes them a favorite and much sought-after pedigreed pet. Abyssinians are medium-sized, lithe, and muscular. Their coats are medium in length—long enough to accommodate two or three bands of ticking—and come in a number of different colors. Wild or agouti-colored and red Abyssinians are most common, whereas blue and beige to fawn-colored ones are rare. The eyes are amber yellow or green.

Point Score for Abyssinians (CFA)

Head (25)	
Muzzle	6
Skull	6
Ears	7
Eye shape	6
Body (30)	
Torso	15
Legs and feet	10
Tail	5
Coat (10)	
Texture	10
Color (35)	
Color	15
Ticking	15
Eye color	5

Manx. Tailless cats are found in many parts of the world. This lack of a tail is a malformation, as I have discussed in connection with the Manx' long-haired relative, the Cymric (page 124). Cats with curly or stunted tails are particularly common in Asia. I myself once had a red curly-tailed cat that was born in Germany but of parents that came from Thailand. The name "Manx" derives from the Isle of Man, the first place in Europe where tailless cats appeared in considerable numbers. Since taillessness is a dominant genetic trait, this race could become established on the Isle of Man. It was then brought to the European continent where one now encounters it at cat shows. I must say, though, that I fail to see why people would want to breed cats with this pathological malformation. On the Isle of Man there are also tailless dogs, but to my knowledge no dog club has attempted to breed them deliberately. The unmistakeable marks of a Manx are the absence of a tail and the resulting weird, hopping gait and raised hindquarters combined with a short back and caved-in sides. Apart from these peculiarities, the Manx resembles the British Shorthair in size and appearance. Coat and eye colors as well as markings are extremely varied since this cat is bred in all the known colors.

Point Score for Manx (CFA)

Head and ears	25
Eyes	5
Body	25
Taillessness	15
Legs and feet	15
Coat	10
Color and markings	5

Burmese. The Burmese is a unicolored cat that is somewhat heavier in build than a Siamese. The first color variety, the Brown Burmese, was imported by Dr. Joseph Thompson of San Francisco to the United States from Burma as a "dark Siamese" and was officially recognized by the CFA in 1936, and in England in 1952. The Burmese is a partial albino with a Burma gene peculiar to this breed (page 98). Today the breed is recognized the world over; it is popular and comes in many colors.

This cat has a medium-sized, elegant, and powerful body that according to the current standard resembles neither the Siamese nor the British Shorthair. The legs are delicate and slender, the head

wedge-shaped, but with the narrow end blunted rather than pointed and somewhat rounded at the top. The chin is well-developed, and there is a slight indentation at the base of the nose. The ears are medium-sized and slightly rounded. The desired eye color is a golden yellow that should be as clear and bright as possible. The fur is supposed to be short and fine and lie close to the body. In all the color varieties, the chest and belly are somewhat lighter than the back and the legs. Ears, face, and legs are a little bit darker than the back.

Although the CFA recognizes only the Brown Burmese, which should have no points coloring, the British Governing Council of the Cat Fancy (GCCF) and the FIFe recognize ten color varieties for Burmese cats: brown, blue, chocolate, lilac, red, brown-tortie, cream, blue-tortie, chocolate-tortie, and lilac-tortie.

Point Score for Burmese (CFA)

Head (25)	
Roundness of head	7
Breadth between eyes	4
Full face with proper profile	8
Ear set and placement	6
Eyes (5)	
Placement and shape	5
Body (30)	
Torso	15
Muscle tone	5
Legs and feet	5
Tail	5
Coat (10)	
Short	4
Close-lying	2
Texture	4
Color (30)	
Body color	25
Eye color	5

Rex Cats. Around 1950 the first Rex cats turned up in Cornwall at the western coast of England. They were small and had short, curly hair. Curly hair is a trait that is passed on in a recessive gene (page 97). A few years later, a curly-haired kitten was born in Devonshire. Genetic experiments revealed that there were two different genetic

House Cats and Pedigreed Cats

strains, and we therefore speak of a Cornish and a Devon Rex. In addition to the English Rex cats, there is a similar mutation that appeared in Germany. These German cats were also born around 1950. They lived in Berlin but were almost all exported. There are a few German breeders who strive to maintain the breed of the German Rex. In the United States, in Italy, and in Australia, too, Rex cats are said to have occurred, but they were not bred there, and the lines died out.

The fur of the Cornish Rex (photograph, page 127) is short, plush-like, thick, and curly or wavy, particularly on the back and the tail. The whiskers and eyebrows are long and curled, too. The body is medium-sized, muscular and solid, but at the same time slender. The legs are long and slender with small, oval feet. The cat looks long-legged. Almost all colors may occur, and at exhibitions one finds even Rex cats with white blazes or Siamese points competing.

The Devon Rex has very short, fine, wavy, and soft fur. The whiskers are curled as in the Cornish Rex. All colors are permitted. The body and legs are similar to those of the Cornish Rex, and the head, which sits on a slender neck, is a squat wedge shape and has prominent cheekbones. The nose has a clear stop, and the line of the forehead bends to form the flat top of the head. The ears are large, sit low on the head, are wide at the base and rounded at the tips and have fine hairs growing on them.

The German variety of Rex cats, which was recognized only recently by the FIFe, has short fur that is reminiscent of mole fur and has an obvious tendency to form waves or curls. The body is strong and muscular, and the cat is larger than the other two Rex varieties. All coat colors are possible, and there are no prescriptions for eye color except that coat and eye color should look attractive together.

•

Point Score for Rex Cats (CFA)

Head (25)	
Size and shape	5
Muzzle and nose	5
Eyes	5
Ears	5
Profile	5

Body (30)	
Size	3
Torso	10
Legs and paws	5
Tail	5
Bone	5
Neck	2
Coat (40)	
Texture	10
Length	5
Wave, extent of wave	20
Close-lying	5
Color (5)	5

Korat. The Korat cat comes from Thailand where it has long played an important role in customs and cultural traditions, and is regarded as a "good luck" cat. Serious breeding of animals imported from Thailand to Europe did not start until 1960. The breed has been recognized by the CFA in the United States. Korat cats have been fairly common in Scandinavia for some time, and they are now getting established in the rest of Europe too, although they are still rare at exhibitions. The Korat is short-haired with a blue-gray coat that has a silver cast to it, is fine, thick, and smooth, and has neither stripes nor differences in shade. The green eye color often develops quite late in kittens. The Korat is a quiet, affectionate cat, with an unusually fine disposition.

Point Score for Korats (CFA)

Head (23)	
Broad head	5
Profile	5
Breadth between eyes	5
Ear set and placement	5
Chin and jaw	3
Eyes (15)	
Size	5
Shape	5
Placement	5
Body (25)	
Body	15

Legs and feet	5
Tail	5
Coat (12)	
Short	4
Texture	4
Close-lying	4
Color (25)	
Body color	20
Eye color	5

Exotic Shorthair. This cat has short, plush-like fur and is intelligent, quiet, and playful. Known in America for twenty years and recognized there about fifteen years ago, Exotic Shorthairs are now finding admirers in Europe, too. With their round, childlike faces and soft fur, they are supposed to correspond in type to Persians, and their coat colors are the same as for Persians.

Nonrecognized Short-haired Breeds

European Shorthair. European Shorthairs differ from British ones only in body build, not in coloration. This breed looks basically the same as an ordinary European house cat that has evolved through natural selection and without human interference. It has a medium-sized, stout body with a well-developed rib cage and is supported by strong legs with solid paws. The head is fairly large, but the face looks long rather than wide. Cheeks and chin are full, and the nose is straight with soft lines and of the same width from the base to the tip. The ears stand up straight and are widely spaced; they are lightly rounded and sometimes have tufts of hair in them. The fur is short, thick, and shiny. The eye colors are the same as for the British Shorthairs, but the coat colors should be pure rather than mixed.

Chartreuse. The Chartreuse is one of the oldest European cat breeds. It is said to have been imported from Africa to France where it was first bred. Supposedly the Carthusian monks, in their monastery "La Grande Chartreuse," took a particular interest in this cat. Its medium-long, solid body is muscular and heavy and the chest broad. The short, sturdy legs have strong, round paws. The pads of the feet and the nose leather are bluish gray, the head broad, the cheeks full, the nose wide and straight, and the ears medium-sized and placed high on the head. The eyes are large, round, and are a bright dark orange as well as clear and expressive. All shades of blue are permitted in the coat, but it is important that the color be uniform and without pattern. The description of the breed indicates that this cat is so similar to the British Blue that the two are easily confused. Even judges and breeders are often at a loss which of the breeds to assign a cat to. Perhaps it would be fair to say that the Chartreuse looks somewhat stouter than the British Blue.

Sphinx. This hairless cat is also the result of genetic mutation. It is bred in the United States and in Europe, but there is little interest in these hairless animals.

Siamese Cats

This breed, which originated in Thailand (Siam), is the best-known purebred cat and is beloved all over the world. The first pair to be used for breeding in England arrived in 1884 and had very little resemblance to today's Siamese cats. Thick, round heads, crossed eyes, and kinks in the tails were the hallmarks of the first Siamese. But these traits were systematically eliminated, and only fine-boned animals with elegant and harmonious lines are now used for breeding. Many people find these highly prized animals too emaciated looking, and they are reluctant to buy cats that seem to be so frail. This may be the reason why in recent years the number of Siamese cats shown at exhibitions has steadily declined.

Siamese cats are especially affectionate and loyal. Their voices sometimes sound like the crying of a baby, and particularly during the heat period their calls can become almost unbearable for the owners, not to mention their neighbors. Neutering puts an end to this unwelcome music. Siamese cats are medium-sized, long, slender, and lithe. They have long, relatively thin legs with the hindlegs somewhat longer than the front legs. The paws are small and oval; the tail, long, straight, and coming to a point; the neck, long and dainty. Body, legs, paws, head, and tail are supposed to be in good propor-

House Cats and Pedigreed Cats

tion to each other, and the overall impression should be one of harmony and elegance. The head is long, the profile should show no break between forehead and nose, and the chin should not be receding. The fur of Siamese is very short, shiny, and fine and lies close to the body. The special feature of Siamese cats is their unusual markings or points (page 114). In Blue-points, the extremities of the body are blue. There are many different colors and some variations in markings, such as the striped Tabby-point and the spotted Tortie-point (recognized only in Europe). There is even a Tortie-Tabby-point Siamese with striped points and cream or red spots superimposed on the tabby markings. The CFA standard, however, includes only the classic colors: seal, chocolate, blue, and lilac. All Siamese have bright blue eyes.

The care of Siamese and Oriental cats is very simple (page 24).

Oriental Shorthairs

Orientals could be described as Siamese cats in unicolored coats. They have no points but are instead the same color all over. Over thirty different color varieties are bred, and this does not include such variations as the Oriental Shorthair Smoke of which I own a young male. Oriental Shorthairs have been created quite recently by crossing Siamese cats with unicolored house cats and then refining the strain through selective breeding. In build, these cats much resemble the Siamese. They are slender, elegant cats, and they are described by fanciers as being "of Oriental type." Well-known varieties are the Havanna or Chestnut, as it is called in the United States (photograph, page 9), which is an Oriental with cigar brown fur, and the Ebony, which is pitch black. All Orientals have clear, bright green eyes, except for the Foreign White, which has blue eyes.

Point Score for Siamese Cats (CFA)

Head (20)	
Long flat profile	6
Wedge, fine muzzle, size	5
Ears	4
Chin	3
Width between eyes	2
Eyes (10)	
Shape, size, slant and placement	10
Body (30)	
Structure and size, including Neck	12
Muscle tone	10
Legs and feet	5
Tail	3
Coat (10)	10
Color (30)	
Body color	10
Point color—matching points of dense color, proper foot pads and nose leather	10
Eye color	10

Point Score for Oriental Shorthairs (CFA)

Head (25)	
Long, flat profile	7
Wedge, fine muzzle, size	6
Ears	5
Chin	4
Width between eyes	3
Eyes (10)	
Shape, size, slant, and placement	10
Body (25)	
Structure and size, including neck	12
Muscle tone	5
Legs and feet	5
Tail	3
Coat (10)	10
Color (30)	
Body color, uniform density of coloring, proper foot pads, and nose leather	20
Eye color	10

Colors and Markings of Various Cat Breeds

Breed	Color designation	Color of coat (ground color)
British Shorthair,	Black	Black, without any gray or brown
Burmese,	Brown	Warm dark brown
European Shorthair,	Chocolate	Warm brown
Exotic Shorthair,	Lilac	Soft lilac with a pink cast
Oriental Shorthair,	White	Pure white
Persians	Blue	Even light blue-gray
	Red	Uniform orange red without markings
	Cream	Light beige pastel, no red
	Black smoke	Silvery white
	Blue smoke	Silvery white
	Red cameo	Pure white
	Red smoke	Silvery white
	Cream cameo	Pure white
	Cream smoke	Silvery white
	Tortoiseshell smoke	Silvery white
	Blue-cream smoke	Silvery white
	Silver tabby	Pure silver
	Silver tabby blue	Pure silver
	Tabby brown	Sand-colored, warm golden brown
	Tabby blue	Ivory
	Tabby red	Red
	Chinchilla	Pure white
	Shaded silver	Pure white
	Tortoiseshell	Light red, dark red, and black
	Tortoiseshell and white	Black and red with white
	Blue tortoiseshell and white	Blue-gray and cream with white
	Black-white	Black and white
	Blue-white	Blue-gray and white
	Red-white	Red and white
	Blue-cream	Light blue-gray and cream mixed
Abyssinian,	Wild or agouti-colored	Brown to orange
Somali	Sorrel	Copper red
Balinese,	Seal-point	Beige
Colorpoint Persian,	Blue-point	Light gray, color of glacier ice
Siamese	Chocolate-point	Ivory colored
	Lilac-point	White
	Red-point	White
	Cream-point	White
	Seal Tortie-point	Beige
	Seal Tabby-point	Beige
Birman	Seal	Eggshell to beige
	Blue	Eggshell to beige

Colors and Markings of Various Cat Breeds

Nose leather	Pads on feet	Pattern*	Rims around eyes & nose
Black	Black or dark brown		
	Dark brown		
Light brown	Cinnamon to light brown		
	Lavender rose		
	Pink		
	Blue-gray		
	Pink or brick red		
	Pink		
	Black or dark brown	Tp black	
	Blue-gray	Tp blue-gray	
	Pink	Tp red	
	Pink	Tp red	
	Pink	Tp cream	
	Pink	Tp cream	
	Pink, black, or mottled red and black	Tp black and red	
	Blue-gray, cream, or mottled blue-gray and cream	Tp blue-gray and cream	
Brick red	Black or dark brown	M black	Black
Brick red	Blue-gray	M blue-gray	Blue-gray
Brick red	Black or dark brown	Tc + M black	Black
Faint pink	Blue-gray	Tc + M blue-gray	Blue-gray
Brick red	Pink	M deep red	Dark red
Brick red	Black or dark brown	Tp black	Black
Brick red	Black or dark brown	Tp black	Black
	Pink, black, or mottled pink and black		
	Pink, black, or mottled pink and black		
	Blue-gray, cream, or mottled blue-gray and cream		
	Pink or black		
	Pink or blue-gray		
	Pink		
	Pink, blue-gray, or mottled pink and blue-gray		
Brick red	Black or brown	Tc black	Black
	Pink	Tc light to reddish brown	Brown
	Dark brown	P dark brown	
	Blue-gray	P blue-gray	
Light brown	Cinnamon to light brown	P light brown	
	Lavender rose	P light gray with pink cast	
	Pink	P light orange	
	Pink	P cream, light beige	
	Pink, dark brown, or mottled pink and dark brown	P dark brown with red spots	
Dark brown or pink	Dark brown	P dark brown striped	Dark brown
Dark brown	Pink or dark brown	P dark brown	
Blue-gray	Pink or blue-gray	P blue-gray	

*P = points; Tc = ticking; Tp = tipping; M = markings

The Relatives of Domestic Cats

All breeds of cats, ranging from the stout Persians to the extremely slender Orientals and including such weird breeds as the Manx and the hairless Sphinx, are basically the same animal: they are house cats, a domesticated form of the European Wild Cat *(Felis silvestris)*. This is why any of these breeds can be crossed with another and produce kittens.

Cats are land-dwelling predators, and the differences between big and small species are relatively small. There are a few minor differences. First, in small cats the hair on the nose does not extend all the way to the tip, as it does in big cats, but stops short and leaves a small bald stripe. Second, small cats consume their prey in a crouching position, whereas big ones lie down to eat. Both of them hold onto the meat or prey with their forepaws while eating.

Big Cats

The group of big cats is made up of two genera: *Panthera,* with six separate members or species (clouded leopard, snow leopard, tiger, leopard, lion and jaguar), and *Acinonyx,* with only one member, the cheetah, which differs from the other big cats in having non-retractable claws and an unusual skull structure.

Panthera

Snow Leopard *(Panthera uncia)*. The snow leopard, measuring about 4½ feet (1.3 meters), is a small member of the family of big cats. It resembles small cats in not being able to roar, something all other big cats can do. Also, its spots are arranged in rows like those of small cats. The dark spots, which lighten up toward the center, are set off clearly against the light gray fur. Snow leopards live at high altitudes above 6,000 feet in the Himalaya Mountains of Central Asia. They are excellent jumpers and can bring down rabbits, sheep, mice, birds, and even deer and other large animals by leaping at them. The fur of snow leopards is wooly and thick, which makes it ideal for the fur industry. Consequently these animals have been hunted almost to the point of extinction.

Tiger *(Panthera tigris)*. The biggest still extant species of cat is the tiger, which can measure up to 9 or 10 feet (2.8 meters). There are eight subspecies of tigers in Southeast Asia, but they are in danger of extinction everywhere. Tigers are strong and muscular, and their yellowish to rust brown coat is covered with black stripes all over the body (tiger markings). The cheek ruff is long, like that of our Persian cats. Neither snow and ice nor water present any problem to tigers because they are excellent swimmers and jumpers, but they are not very good at climbing. Because of their extraordinary strength they can kill even horses and young elephants. Tigers are solitary animals, but at mating time they form close family ties. The young are born after a gestation period of about 110 days. They are weaned after about six months but do not leave their mother until they are two or three years old.

Lion *(Panthera leo)*. It is easy to tell a male lion from a female one because the male has a mane. The coat of a lion is sand-colored like the desert, without spots or stripes. The lion's impressive and almost majestic looks, as well as his resounding roar, inspire respect and fear and this "king of beasts" is a prominent figure in both myth and heraldry. In many parts of the world it has been hunted out of existence, and only in some national parks in Africa — primarily in Serengeti National Park in East Africa — do lions still live in larger groups and relatively undisturbed. Females live in groups, or prides, that stay together for life and usually also include anywhere from one to six sexually mature males. It happens quite frequently that these lords are attacked and driven away by other males that do not belong to a pride. When they reach sexual maturity at about four years, male lions leave their pride to find hunting grounds of their own. The females temporarily leave the pride to mate and give birth to their cubs. Gestation takes about 110 days, and a litter consists of two to four cubs, which can weigh up to 3 pounds (1.5 kilograms). The cubs nurse for six months. Later, the females stay with the pride, whereas the males leave when they reach maturity. In zoos lions sometimes mate with other big cats such as tigers and leopards.

The Relatives of Domestic Cats

Leopard *(Panthera pardus)*. Leopards, too, are threatened with extinction in the last areas where they are still found. There are leopards in Africa, southern Asia, and China; in northern Africa, where they used to thrive, they are extinct. Leopards are very modest in their demands and can find prey in both dry steppes and wet forests. They are slender, somewhat over 3 feet (1 meter) long, and have yellowish to reddish coats that are covered with dark spots. The spots on the back have a light center (darker than the ground color); the rest of the body has black spots. The twenty-four subspecies vary from each other only in minor respects like fur color and size. There are also totally black leopards (due to the presence of a melanistic gene) that are called black panthers. Leopards live together only during mating season; otherwise they are solitary. Males help feed the young, which reach full maturity only at three to four years.

Jaguar *(Panthera onca)*. Jaguars differ from leopards primarily in being larger, heavier, and stronger. The coat is reddish, and the rings on it are larger than those of leopards and often have dark dots in the middle. There are six subspecies, all of which are found in the southwestern United States and in Central America. Jaguars live in forests and steppes and hunt mostly on the ground because — being less lithe than other cats — they are not good climbers. Jaguars kill all sorts of mammals ranging from mice to deer and also prey on birds and frogs. The young are born after a gestation period of 95 to 105 days. They weigh about one pound at birth and open their eyes after nine days, like house cats. Males help raise the young by providing prey. A jaguar is fully mature at about three years.

Acinonyx

Cheetah *(Acinonyx jubatus)*. Cheetahs are lighter, more slender, and longer-legged than leopards. They cannot withdraw their claws. The coat is often yellow on the back and sides and white on the underside. The entire body is covered with round, black spots, and the end of the tail has black rings and a white tip. The ears are small and rounded at the tips, and the eyes are yellowish brown. The cheetah's natural habitat is the dry savanna. It used to be common all over Africa and in some areas of the Near East and of India. Today significant populations are left only in Iran and in southern and western Africa. Cheetahs are extinct in India.

Cheetahs can be tamed and learn to accept humans as their masters in about six months. They were used as early as 1200 B.C. by the Egyptians to help them on hunts.

Cheetahs are fabulous runners. It has been estimated that they can reach speeds of up to 65 miles (110 kilometers) per hour. They live primarily on gazelles, antelopes, rabbits, hares, rodents, and birds. They kill their prey with a bite in the throat after a swift chase. Male cheetahs help in raising the cubs. The baby cheetahs open their eyes at eight to eleven days and are weaned after six weeks. The mother often moves her brood, something I have also observed in my pedigreed and ordinary house cats. This keeps the lair clean and free of smells so that enemies cannot spot it as easily. It is difficult to breed cheetahs in captivity, but a few zoos have succeeded in this attempt, and we may thus hope that this threatened species will not die out.

Small Cats

All parts of the world except for Australia have small native cats. The group of small cats, which is made up of fifteen genera and twenty-eight species, includes relatively large animals like the puma and little ones like the Black-footed cat. The best known ones among them — and those of greatest interest to us here — are the wildcats, from which our house cats are descended.

In adapting to their environments, three subgroups of wildcats have evolved: the Indian Desert cat, the European wildcat, and the African wildcat.

Indian Desert cats *(Felis rubiginosa)*. These live mostly in bushy and grassy steppes in the warm, dry regions of the Near East. These cats' fur is soft and dense and sand-colored with spots.

European wildcats *(Felis silvestris)*. These forest cats occur in Europe and the cooler parts of western Eurasia. They are yellowish gray with dark, silvery stripes, and their tails are short and ringed

The Relatives of Domestic Cats

with a very dark tip. It is possible for house cats to mate with these cats — matings of female housecats with wild males are most likely — but in the long run the traits of the wildcat, representing a better genetic adaptation, always reassert themselves, so that the population of wildcats remains essentially the same in genetic make-up.

African wildcat *(Felis lybica).* This cat is relatively small and slender with large ears and a long tail. It came to Europe from Africa in the early Middle Ages, and it was some time before it became commonly accepted as a domestic cat. All the shapes and colors of house cats we have today go back to this cat. People often claim that the sturdy build and various coat colors of some cats were produced by crossing domestic cats with the European wildcat, but there is no conclusive evidence for this view. On the contrary, it seems very unlikely that the genes of wildcats significantly influenced the population of domestic cats. In African wildcats there exists a considerable variety of builds and colors, and it thus seems quite likely that the different types of modern housecats resulted simply from domestication of African wildcats. Our purebred Abyssinians (page 129) would seem to come closest in appearance to their ancestor, the Nubian African wildcat.

African Desert cat *(Felis margarita).* In the desert areas of Africa and the Near East, a special type of wildcat developed, namely the African Desert cat or Sandcat. It has a broader head than other small cats and large, wide ears. Its sense of hearing is remarkable. The coat and its markings make it clear that this is a relative of the wildcat.

Chinese Desert or **Gobi cat** *(Felis beiti).* This cat lives in the Far East, where it inhabits brushy areas, steppes, mountain areas, and open forests in Central Asia.

Black-footed cat *(Felis nigripes).* Another relative of the wildcat is the Black-footed cat. This is the smallest of all the African cats with a body length (excluding the tail) of no more than 14 to 18 inches (35 to 46 cm). It lives in South Africa in dry, sandy plains and savannahs.

Jungle cat *(Felis chans).* This cat is also related to wildcats, and developed into a species of its own earlier than other small cats. This cat's head is longer and more pointed than that of other wildcats, and the ears are pointed and equipped with tufts. These cats occur in North Africa and Asia.

There are three different species of Golden cats, each of which is named according to the geographical area where it is found.

African Golden cat *(Felis aurata).* Living in the high deciduous forests of western and central Africa, it resembles our European wildcat in its habits, hunting primarily on the ground. It is somewhat less tall than the Serval cat, and its coat can be sand-colored, red, or even black, either with spots or unicolored, or with markings restricted to eye spots and stripes on the legs.

Temminck's Golden cat *(Felis temmincki).* This cat lives in the forests of eastern Asia and feeds on fair-sized rodents, small deer, and all kinds of birds. This cat also has various coat colors and patterns, and a gray patch behind each ear.

Bornean Red or **Bay cat** *(Felis badia).* This type of Golden cat is smaller than the two previously mentioned species, and its skull is shorter and rounder.

Leopard *(Felis bengalensis).* Found in southern Asia, this is the most common of the three species of leopard cats. The fur is a light ochre or silvery gray and has lovely and striking markings. Stripes on the head and nape of the neck, several rows of dark spots running down the back, rings with light centers on the sides, bands on the throat, and spotted legs and tail make up the picture of this handsome cat. There are seven subspecies.

Rusty-spotted cat *(Felis rubiginosa).* This close relative of the Leopard cat is found in southern India and Sri Lanka. It resembles the Leopard cat closely, but is smaller, only 17 inches (43 cm) long.

Fishing cat *(Felis viverrinus).* Larger than the Leopard, the Fishing cat is at home in India, southern China, on the greater Sudda Islands, and

The Relatives of Domestic Cats

on Sri Lanka. Although it is called the "fishing" cat, it lives primarily on rodents, snakes, birds, and smaller aquatic creatures like frogs and mollusks.

Flat-headed cat *(Felis planiceps).* There is only one species of Flat-headed cat. Its reddish-brown coat is almost without markings. It has a long body, short legs, a short tail, a flat skull, and a slightly up-turned nose. This is the only small cat that can pull up but not retract its claws. Another peculiarity is its very sharp teeth. This cats lives close to water in Southeast Asia, primarily on Borneo and Sumatra. It eats fish, frogs, fruit, and sweet potatoes.

The Marbled cat *(Felis marmorata).* This cat lives in the forests of the Far East and of Sumatra and Borneo. The coat of this cat exhibits various shades of gray with large, rimmed patches similar to those of the clouded leopard. The paws and parts of the tail are spotted. There are two subspecies.

There are five members in the ocelot family, beautiful spotted animals, all of which are, unfortunately, in danger of dying out.

Ocelot *(Felis pardalis).* The most threatened is the Ocelot, which has been, and continues to be, hunted to an irresponsible degree. In spite of many campaigns to enlighten the public, the beautifully marked fur of the ocelot is still being made into fur coats. The home of this animal is in the thorny chaparral, rocks and dense, humid forests of Central America as well as of North and South America, areas where it used to be abundant. Ocelots like to climb trees and sleep there.

Tree Ocelot, or **Margay** *(Felis wiedi).* Also called "Little Ocelot," it looks just like the regular ocelot but is considerably smaller. It lives exclusively in the forests in the same geographical areas as the regular ocelot. Its remarkable climbing skills surpass those of any other cats. The anatomical structure of this species' hindlegs differs from that of other cats and is responsible for the extraordinary agility and rotational capacity of the legs.

Geoffrey's cat *(Felis geoffroyi).* There are five subspecies of Geoffrey's cat, all of which occur in southern South America. They resemble the Tree ocelot in size and overall appearance but have smaller dots. They love water and are said to be good swimmers.

Chilean Forest cat or **Kodkod** *(Felis guigua).* In spite of its name, this cat often lives in the open steppes of Chile and Patagonia. Its coat is very dark, and the round black spots on it are very heavy. The tail is short. This cat lives on mice, rats, guinea pigs, and birds.

Pampas cat *(Felis colocolo).* From southern South America, this cat inhabits open plateaus and pampas, and hunts rodents, birds, and lizards. It has long hair, with colors and markings that differ widely. The size of this animal corresponds to that of our housecats.

Andean cat *(Felis jacobita).* This cat is a species all its own and is also found in South America, where it lives in arid mountainous regions, occasionally above the snow line. It is often confused with the Pampas cat, not because the two cats resemble each other, but because very few people have ever seen a true Andean cat.

Jaguarundi *(Felis yagouaroundi).* The jaguarundi has eight subspecies, and is often called the weasel cat, although it looks more like an otter. It is found in Central and South America and in the southern United States, where it hunts small rodents, rabbits, birds, and fish.

Pallas cat or **Manill** *(Felis manul).* The Manill does not belong to the wildcats but is closely related to them. It resembles our housecats somewhat, and —because of its soft, thick fur—looks plump and stocky. It lives in central Asia, where there are also some variants that developed in adaptation to local conditions.

Serval cat *(Felis serva).* Its fourteen subspecies always live near the water. With its body length of about 32 inches (80 centimeters), this cat should really be counted among the medium-sized cats. Its fur is sand-colored with irregular, large, dark patches that dot the whole body. This cat is found

The Relatives of Domestic Cats

almost throughout Africa where it preys on rodents, birds, hares, and young antelopes.

At this point lynxes are divided into only two species, the Northern lynx, and the bobcat. In earlier days, the Caracal was counted among the lynxes too.

Northern lynx *(Felis lynx).* This lynx used to be common from Europe to Siberia. It is medium-sized, has a short tail, and varies in coat pattern according to locality. There are almost unicolored animals as well as strikingly spotted ones. The lynx lives in the forested parts of northern America and occasionally still in northern Eurasia. The lynx's most noticeable feature is his large, tufted ears which contribute to this animal's proverbial acuity of hearing.

Bobcat *(Felis rufus).* The bobcat has somewhat shorter ear tufts and a smaller body. Its area of distribution is southern Canada, the United States, and southern and eastern Mexico. The bobcat is still quite common in the United States where it can be found in all kinds of habitats, like chaparral, forests, subtropical swamps, mountains, and even semi-deserts.

Caracal lynx *(Felis caracal).* This cat is not, truly speaking, a lynx, but it is related to it. The caracal is slender and dainty; its color ranges from red to yellowish gray; and it has no spots on its body but does have ear tufts. It lives in Africa and Asia in nine subspecies. In the hot times of the year it retreats to rock crannies and caves abandoned by other animals.

Puma *(Felis concolor).* Although the Puma measures as much as 5 feet and more (1.6 m), it is classed with the small cats. Its coat color ranges from red to brownish gray and silver gray, with dark rust red being the most common. There are also black specimens. In many areas of northern America, the puma has been almost totally eradicated, but there are still regions in Canada and the United States where the puma occurs with some frequency. In South America, it is threatened with extinction. Pumas adapt to almost all types of landscape ranging from tropical rain forests to high mountains, and they hunt whatever is available: everything from mice and birds to deer and young bears. The care of the young is entirely up to the mother, because the male takes no interest in this chore.

Clouded Leopard *(Panthera nebulosa).* Although it resembles the Marbled cat in build and coat pattern, it weighs four to ten times as much as that smaller cat. The Clouded Leopard has extraordinarily long canines. Because of its short legs and its climbing skills it can move with great agility in branches and prefers living in trees. It inhabits the forests of China, Indochina, Sumatra, and Borneo. In contrast to most other small cats, which give birth after a gestation of sixty to seventy days (sixty-three for house cats), the gestation period of Clouded Leopards is ninety days.

For Reference

Cat Associations and Their Addresses

American Cat Association, Inc.
  Susie Page
  10065 Foothill Boulevard
  Lake View Terrace, CA 91342

American Cat Fanciers' Association, Inc.
  Edward Rugenstein
  P.O. Box 203
  Point Lookout, MO 65726

Canadian Cat Association
  Donna Aragona
  14 Nelson Street W., Suite 5
  Brampton, Ontario
  Canada L6X 1B7

Cat Fanciers' Association, Inc.
  Walter A. Friend, Jr.
  1309 Allaire Avenue
  Ocean, NJ 07712

Cat Fanciers' Federation, Inc.
  Barbara Haley
  9509 Montgomery Road
  Cincinnati, OH 45242

Crown Cat Fanciers' Federation
  Martha Underwood
  1379 Tyler Park Drive
  Louisville, KY 40204

International Cat Association
  Bob Mullen
  211 East Olive, Suite 201
  Burbank, CA 91502

United Cat Federation, Inc.
  David Young
  6621 Thornwood Street
  San Diego, CA 92111

Cat Publications

Animals Magazine
  MSPCA
  350 South Huntington Avenue
  Boston, MA 02130

The Cat Fanciers' Almanac
  Cat Fanciers' Association
  1309 Allaire Avenue
  Ocean, NJ 07712

Cat Fancy Magazine
  P.O. Box 2431
  Boulder, CO 80321

Cats Magazine
  P.O. Box 83048
  Lincoln, NE 68501

CFA Yearbook
  Cat Fanciers' Association
  1309 Allaire Avenue
  Ocean, NJ 07712

Index

Italics indicate color photographs

Index

Index